Marcia Ballinger, PhD

Make the
jump

REINVENT YOUR CAREER
IN THE NONPROFIT SECTOR

MAKE THE JUMP
Reinvent Your Career in the Nonprofit Sector

Copyright © 2021 by Marcia Ballinger

ISBN: 978-0-9981779-9-1

Printed in the United States of America

Designed by Ivan Stojic

First Printing: 2021

ARTISAN
DIGITAL

651-600-0178

To my husband, Brad,
a savvy consultant to the nonprofit sector

and

To our daughter, Analisa,
a promising nonprofit executive

What people are saying about
Make the Jump...

"Making a difference requires a pivot to new priorities and plans. This book is your jumping-off point and a handy, insightful roadmap to forge your new career as a difference-maker in the nonprofit sector."

Joseph Daniel McCool

Author of *Deciding Who Leads* and Founder, The McCool Group

"Marcia Ballinger has filled a big gap in the market for career transition advice: the proven nitty gritty of successfully moving from corporate to nonprofit sector. Separating myth from reality, this is a stellar guide for those who are committed to the nonprofit path."

Peggy Bier

President, The Career Development Team

"This is a masterpiece for anyone who is serious about a JUMP from the corporate to nonprofit sector."

Christopher J. King, PhD, MHSc, FACHE

Chair, Health Systems Administration, Georgetown University

"When I was making my own JUMP from big time college athletic coaching, 'reinventing' myself, Marcia helped me with my next chapter. With her guidance and support, I built a consulting business that is soaring, a nonprofit organization that is amazing, and currently serve on three boards. Make sure you read this book."

Pam Borton

ICF PCC Senior Executive Coach, Global Executive Team Coach, Professional Speaker, Author

"This is one of those go-to books on your shelf that will be highlighted in yellow and the pages dog-eared. I guarantee that you'll reference before every informational meeting, interview, and call with recruiter if you are thinking about doing meaningful work that impacts lives in the nonprofit sector."

Anne Pryor

LinkedIn Expert, Career Coach, Lovitude Soul Painter

"I'm going to be giving *Make the Jump* as gifts to people I mentor and coach. High value, great advice. Ballinger has done it again. A must read!"

Cyndi Lesher

Retired Energy Executive, Community Volunteer and Philanthropist

"Countless executives, including me, have called Marcia Ballinger to get advice during a career transition. This book extends access to her practical and direct wisdom to everyone."

Scott Burns

CEO and Co-Founder, Structural

"As someone who 'jumped,' I can attest that Marcia's wisdom and experience are profoundly helpful. Read this book to navigate your job search with your eyes wide open! I did and never looked back."

Susan Adams Loyd

CEO, Better Business Bureau, Minnesota & North Dakota

"For 34 years, I have valued Marcia's counsel on many topics. For anyone considering making the 'jump' from the corporate world to the nonprofit sector, jump **immediately** and read this book. A wealth of wisdom."

Jeff Prouty

Chairman and Founder, The Prouty Project Inc.

"Marcia Ballinger has written a must-read and must-follow book for all who are considering moving from the business world into a leadership role in non-profits. Her connections and stories will resonate with each turn of the page."

Diana Pierce

News Anchor (retired); Host, What's Next: For Those Past 50 From Those Past 50

"If you are considering changing industries for your next career move and targeting the nonprofit sector, THIS BOOK IS FOR YOU!!!"

Karen Bullesbach

Senior Vice President, Professional Services, LHH

"There is nothing simple about either of the two topics in this book: changing careers or leading nonprofit organizations. Marcia has made both subjects appealing and approachable. I'm excited about this book because the world needs good leaders to join and effectively lead nonprofits."

Paul Batz

Founder and CEO, Good Leadership

"Many need to keep earning an income, but they also want work that more directly reflects their values and beliefs. How to make the transition? Marcia Ballinger taps into her many years of experience to offer readers a practical blueprint."

Chris Farrell

Marketplace Senior Economics Contributor, American Public Media Group

"A **must-read** for anyone considering a career transition to the nonprofit sector. Read this book and get to yes!"

Anne Chang

Vice President Human Capital, UnitedHealth Group

"Marcia is our go-to resource for helping those who want to move into nonprofit leadership roles. Incredible advice!"

Anne deBruin Sample

CEO, Navigate Forward

"What a book! If you have found yourself wondering how to translate years of corporate experience into leading in the nonprofit sector, this is for you."

Eric Black

President and CEO, Minnesota Diversified Industries (MDI)

Foreword

I had my first conversation with Dr. Marcia Ballinger nearly 15 years ago. It was a phone call and as we hung up, I remember feeling equally intimidated and welcomed by someone so proficient in their subject matter expertise (career coaching and executive recruitment) yet equally empathetic to the questions I was posing about how I might make a career "jump" into the business of executive search. During that 20-minute phone call, I experienced her patience, compassion, sense of humor, and ability to share unexpected or difficult feedback in a way that could be heard and absorbed by the recipient.

In the 15 years that followed, I've been privileged to work alongside Marcia as a partner and co-founder and personally overhear (the gift of an open office space) thousands of similar coaching conversations between Marcia and leaders seeking her counsel at moments of pivotal potential career transformation. Thousands of strangers have called Marcia during her weekly open office hours and invited her into their career inner circle—where vocation, identity, values, and conflicting priorities collide—to hear her perspective, counsel, and questions to consider as they navigate making a critical career decision.

Sometimes it's a decision to leave or stay in an unfulfilling, but highly compensated, leadership role.

Sometimes it's a decision to stay in or step out of an interview process that increasingly illuminates serious gaps in values and/or mutual expectations.

Sometimes it's a decision to actively pursue a new leadership role filled with unknowns, uncertainty, and fluid organizational dynamics.

Whatever the situation, Marcia's reputation as a trusted coach, counselor, and safe harbor for reflection is one I will vouch for with every fiber of my being. You can trust what she's sharing because she's passing it along directly from leaders who took a risk in reaching out to an unknown counselor and sharing their innermost reflections on their own leadership transitions.

If you're picking up this book, you've likely arrived at the edge of your known world and are seeking resources to help you navigate the unknown ahead. Friend, you've made a great investment. The ROI on this book won't end when the pages do. This is an author who welcomes ongoing connection and conversation with those who seek her counsel, so don't let that opportunity go to waste. Reach out and share what you've learned from the lessons, counsel, and examples in the pages to come and you'll be contributing to the growth and development of a peer network that stretches across the globe.

As you contemplate making your own leap, I hope you'll find in these pages the insight, counsel, and courage to take flight.

I can speak from 15 years of partnership that Marcia's an exceptional co-pilot to invite along for the ride ahead.

Onwards and upwards!!

Lars-Erik B. Leafblad

Table of Contents

CHAPTER ONE

The Compelling Question

A few years back, a local consultant and I were discussing how to manage our steady streams of calls from people looking for advice. My friend is *the* guru on creating a LinkedIn profile that gets noticed and conveys a career narrative in the best possible light. Her phone rang at all times of day from folks with "a quick question" about improving their online brand. She didn't want to slight these inquiries, yet she needed to prioritize the needs of paying clients.

So each week, she blocked out a specific time when anyone could call about anything. Maybe LinkedIn. Or just to say hello. Questions big or small. She tackled it all.

Accessibility matters to my friend, and she widely advertises her availability. Each caller gets a warm welcome.

People with general questions were now much more likely to dial during her specified hour. Fewer interruptions. Better concentration. Higher likelihood the caller will get through and get help. Win-Win!

Genius Idea. So I stole it.

Each week, I block out an hour and a half to take random phone calls. I've usually never met the callers. I promise confidentiality, and I invite people to talk about anything they wish.

I've dubbed my hour each Wednesday from 8 a.m. to 9:30 a.m. "The Recruiter Is IN," a nod to Lucy's sidewalk therapy stand in the classic *Peanuts* comic strip, a favorite of mine for its nuggets of wisdom as well as the childhood connection of its creator, Charles Schulz, to our home neighborhood in St. Paul, Minnesota.

Because of my professional background, questions usually involve job search. I've been a co-founder and partner at two executive search firms and have worked in the industry for nearly 25 years. In the past, I've specialized in corporate search, recruiting leaders to roles in finance, manufacturing, engineering, and human resources in companies from small technology start-ups to international conglomerates. Today, I specialize in the nonprofit sector, recruiting leaders to organizations in social services, philanthropy, higher education, and health care. At times, I've recruited simultaneously in both the for-profit and nonprofit sectors.

Along the way, I've looked at tens of thousands of resumes and applications. I've interviewed thousands of talented professionals from all over the country, indeed, from all over the world, assessing the candidates against the requirements for specific positions. I've called countless references to gather even more information about candidates from people who have worked with them most closely.

In short, I've become known as someone who knows and can speak to the job transition process. Hence, "The Recruiter is IN."

I started these weekly sessions five years ago, and they're still going strong.

My call-in time is almost always packed. I manage to have productive conversations with three to five people per week. Because I can give each caller my full attention, I truly enjoy the conversations.

I set the stage by welcoming the caller to share whatever is on their mind. I'm open to discussing anything from resumes to interviews and everything in between.

In theory, the calls can represent any number of topics.

Except—they don't.

One compelling question has dominated "The Recruiter Is IN" from the day it launched:

"I'm a corporate executive and I would like to move into the nonprofit sector. *How do I make the jump?*"

Listen in on some typical calls:

VERNON is an Enterprise Risk Advisor for a large east coast financial services organization. His 25-year career has focused on risk management, and he teaches risk management for a regional training organization.

Connecting with me via LinkedIn, Vernon sent a note asking for a call or a meeting. He believes nonprofits could be an option for his next position. Not seeing any reference to nonprofit volunteerism or involvement on his LinkedIn profile, it isn't clear to me how Vernon's background connects to roles in the nonprofit sector.

DIANDRA was referred to me by a recruiter friend in Chicago aware of our focus on finding leaders for nonprofits. Diandra's resume outlined a background of early experiences leading political campaigns and later leadership roles in state government agencies. She's interested in moving out of state government to a health care organization, nonprofit organization, or corporate government affairs department. How serious is she about nonprofit work compared to other sectors? I would have to find out.

GINA, a childhood friend of my next-door neighbor, acted as Clerk of the Bankruptcy Court for the District of New Mexico for many years. An unexpected job loss left her reeling.

Gina contacted me to understand how her work might translate into the nonprofit sector. I didn't have great news for her. I suggested a career in bankruptcy law and bankruptcy court clerkships would likely only translate to a very few nonprofit organizations—legal aid, perhaps. However, I encouraged her to reflect on the parts of the nonprofit community where she already had connections and to pose the question to leaders in the field. Maybe there was something out there I was missing. Her network could help answer the question.

MIKKEL called me late one afternoon. He expected to leave a voicemail and was surprised when I picked up. Mikkel shared his work experience, more than 25 years in information technology, including large scale data warehouse design and management for two of the largest insurance companies in the Unites States as well as a stint doing similar work in Ireland.

Mikkel also shared his avocational work as caretaker and ad-vocate for his youngest sister, who was living with a brain injury. In this role, Mikkel had significant personal experience with state, county, local government, and nonprofit supports for individuals like his sister coping with cognitive disabilities. Mikkel wondered if his lived experience qualified him to move into a nonprofit orga-nization. Indeed, he thought he might have the right stuff to run a nonprofit serving individuals with disabilities. What did I think?

FRANK emailed me and followed up with a call. He shared his disappointment at limited responses to his applications for senior marketing and communications roles.

Looking at Frank's resume, I saw a long career in marketing, primarily in print news. His most recent role included online and social media marketing for a large regional newspaper, but he was laid off as the paper cut costs at the executive level. What to do now? Frank told me he had been extremely busy with an unpredictable schedule the last several years, and not able to connect with the nonprofit sector. But, he said, he was ready now. "I want to have my last chapter be about giving back."

Frank had been applying for various nonprofit leadership roles without success. "What's wrong with these organizations?" he asked.

Like these callers, you feel drawn to consider joining the nonprofit sector. That's terrific! The nonprofit sector needs the involvement and investment of a broad array of community members. The tug you feel to serve in the nonprofit sector is a positive thing.

What's a Nonprofit?

It might sound strange, but many people are confused about what a nonprofit actually is. Sure, a nonprofit is technically an organization that "doesn't make a profit," but let's face it, there are plenty of organizations of all types that don't make money. And if a nonprofit organization doesn't know how to create revenue streams and stay in the black, it won't exist for long. The term "not-for-profit," used interchangeably with "nonprofit," simultaneously clarifies and muddies the waters.

I often talk with people about their perceptions of the nonprofit world. In doing so, I encounter recurring misperceptions:

Nonprofit organizations have a mission.
Yes, but so do for-profit organizations. Most have mission statements. They're usually positive, lofty sentences meant to capture the hearts and minds of employees, customers, and community. As circumstances change,

mission statements are formally created, shared, and often updated. They may be, as in the case of Medtronic, as core to the organization as to any nonprofit: "To contribute to human welfare by application of biomedical engineering in the research, design, manufacture, and sale of instruments or appliances that alleviate pain, restore health, and extend life." Obviously, there's a financial component. But what noble goals!

Nonprofit organizations are full of great people.

So are for-profit organizations. Every organization, whether for-profit or nonprofit, has a unique culture. Unique staff. Unique leadership. You'll find talented, committed people in all types of organizations.

Nonprofit organizations are simple.

Nope. Many nonprofit organizations have multiple programs and multiple revenue streams, making them just as complex as many for-profit organizations. Our firm has a nonprofit client that provides more than 20 categories of program services in over 100 locations. Revenue comes from multiple contracts at the federal, state, and county levels, along with earned income and numerous philanthropic sources. Hardly simple. All organizations, whether a global conglomerate or a start-up, have complexity. It's just choosing which type of complexity is right for you.

Nonprofit organizations aren't concerned about money.

Any nonprofit leader would chuckle at that! Nonprofit organizations must meet budgets and pay bills just like all other organizations. While nonprofits don't pay income taxes, they're responsible for state and property taxes. Revenue might come from government contracts, programmatic income, donations, grants, or any number of other sources. Indeed, there may be *more* concern about money at a nonprofit as resources for "extras" can sometimes be hard to find.

I spoke to a packaging engineer recently who told me he had his sights set on making a career change. When I asked what type of organizational role he was seeking, he shared that he was open to various positions, "but

I want to get into a nonprofit." I asked if he could be more specific. Nope, he said, he just wanted to work in a "nonprofit."

I had to tell him that was like asking advice about getting into a "for-profit." Not much to go on.

There's great variety within the nonprofit sector. As wide a span as the difference between your local Little League baseball team or the World Wildlife Fund or the International Red Cross and Red Crescent Societies. Organizations differ in size, geographic scope, and purpose. The types of nonprofit organizations are practically infinite.

Within the classification of "nonprofit," you'll find:

- hospitals and health care providers
- schools and institutions of higher education
- social service organizations
- religious and faith-based organizations
- trade and professional associations
- foundations, including private and community foundations
- chambers of commerce
- economic development and community development endeavors
- organizations providing housing and services for older adults and individuals with disabilities
- theatres and concert halls
- museums and art institutions
- amateur sports organizations
- and on and on...

So what's the real difference? Other than tax status, is there anything that truly separates nonprofit from for-profit? What attributes are unique to nonprofits?

It's hard to generalize, but most nonprofit organizations typically do share the following characteristics, making them different from most for-profits:

- **Without profit as a driver**, nonprofit organizations manage budgets to achieve a variety of program or service objectives.

- Decision-making and problem-solving usually encompass **a broader set of stakeholders**, including the community.

- **Collaborative processes**, inclusive of many perspectives, are highly valued.

- Leaders of nonprofits never have financial ownership in the organization the way for-profit leaders often do. They are **drawn to the work of the organization for other reasons.**

- Nonprofit organizations are often **more intentional about hiring staff members who reflect the communities served** and about cultural competence as a value in the organization's culture.

- Nonprofit **compensation ranges** are less than pay rates for comparable jobs at for-profits.

- Nonprofits **fill needs the private sector has left behind and the public sector struggles to meet.**

The Nonprofit Appeal

There was a time when the missions now carried out by charitable nonprofit organizations were addressed by various levels of government, by religious organizations, and even by the private sector, as when factories were built in specific communities to bring economic stability and vitality to the area. Today, however, government spending is stretched thin, religious institutions struggle to keep their doors open, and the private sector has, for the most part, long abandoned social benefit in favor of shareholder wealth.

Therefore:

The need for nonprofit organizations is arguably greater now than it ever has been.

Their appeal resonates with a workforce that wants more than a paycheck from its investment of knowledge and skills.

This attraction is especially true among executives and other leaders in the public sector or in government.

The nonprofit sector is a real deal. Over one and a half million nonprofit organizations are registered in the United States with the Internal Revenue Service (IRS). The sector contributes more than $1 trillion (with a "t") to the US economy, comprising over 5 percent of the country's gross domestic product (GDP).

Included in that 1.5 million number of nonprofit organizations are a diverse group of entities involved in a variety of social services, the arts, health care, education, advocacy, labor unions, business and professional associations, and more.

From faith communities to cultural centers to food shelves, nonprofit organizations employ over 10 million people, not counting another 63 million people who work for them on a volunteer basis.

Nonprofits and other organizations have worked mightily to change delivery methods in the face of changing circumstances such as the COVID-19 pandemic. They've had to figure out how to reach people with, in many cases, very personal services, while not being able to physically interact. They are attempting to walk the fine line of asking for increased donations at a time when they are aware that some donors may be stretched and tapped out financially themselves.

Yet, their work has never been more important.

Nonprofit organizations do good. They serve, they teach, they provide care. Nonprofit organizations house unwanted animals. They offer artistic programs to challenge and entertain. They coach displaced workers on new and relevant job skills. The list of interesting and meaningful services and programs nonprofit organizations provide is almost endless. You're probably personally connected with many such organizations yourself.

If you're moved by the good work being done by nonprofit organizations in your community, or even around the world, that's great!

In the nonprofit world, you'll meet like-minded partners, and you'll discover there's little in life more magnetic than people committed to helping other people.

And the more you learn about the nonprofit sector, the more impressed you'll be. You'll find organizations from one-person single-objective organizations serving a specific population in a small geography to large NGOs providing a multitude of programs to populations around the globe.

Make Your Jump

Executives rarely call me looking to spend a "middle chapter" or "mid-career chapter" in a nonprofit.

For example, I contacted a highly talented corporate strategy executive, Ben, about a role as CEO of a regional economic development organization.

Ben was intrigued, agreeing that he possessed both the right experience and a passion for the entity's mission. In the end, however, Ben respectfully declined to be considered for the job. He definitely wanted to lead a nonprofit—someday. But it was too soon. "I'm still in the middle of my corporate 'never come back' career!" he told me. "If I take a job in nonprofit now, I will have to stay there and not be able to come back."

The phrases I hear most often from corporate executives looking at nonprofit roles are these:

My next chapter
My last chapter
My third chapter
My final chapter

And

I want to give back
I want to be mission driven
I want to serve

Over and over, I hear some combination of these words:

It's my final chapter and I want to give back.
I want my third chapter to be mission driven.
For the last chapter of my career,
I would like to be of service to others.

I have to be honest. While such sentiments are noble, and even sincere, I've watched many well-meaning business leaders falter on the way to a nonprofit role.

Here's how it usually goes:

- Many corporate executives rush to look at nonprofit opportunities with little preparation. They don't understand where their background might best fit. They fail to engage their network to assist them in preparing for the transition.

- They apply for several jobs (often unsuited to their background) and get frustrated by a lack of response. Their applications in the for-profit sector generate interest and responses so they follow up on those. They drop the pursuit of a nonprofit position.

- Other corporate folks leverage their network to initiate conversations about joining the nonprofit sector. They get opportunities to talk with nonprofits about possible roles. But they bring an attitude of entitlement (*"Now*, I want a job where I can be mission driven") or condescension ("I'll bring *best practices* from my business career to improve your organization") toward the sector that doesn't resonate. They don't get far in the interview process.

- Most people coming from corporate to nonprofit seek roles that are unreasonable for their background ("I want to be an Executive Director!") and therefore don't get many opportunities to interview.

Yet a few people do make the jump. They keep at it until they get the role they seek. And I've found that superstars in business can be superstars in nonprofit.

Probably the most important characteristic of these leaders is they bring a healthy sense of self-understanding and humility. They know what they know—and they know what they don't know. They're comfortable in their own skin and don't mind asking for help. They're transparent in their thinking, and they collaborate with others. If hired as the head of a nonprofit, they're wise and genuine ambassadors of the mission. They can tell a story and ask for resources. They can run complex organizations with care and decisiveness—simultaneously!

If you're drawn to the mission of nonprofit organizations, I'm happy to help you embark on a journey to discover what's possible. The goal of this book is to give you insights into *if* and *how* to make the jump to a nonprofit leadership role.

When business leaders ask me about a move to a nonprofit role, I caution that the opportunities at a leadership level are highly competitive and much tougher to win than they might anticipate. As you consider making your own jump, remember the difference between a reckless climbing accident and a magnificent cliff dive is where and how you land. So look before you leap!

To get started, I want to spotlight those who made the jump and landed beautifully. I trust you'll be inspired by their stories and benefit from what they learned along the way.

CHAPTER TWO

Spotlights on Success

Your career story is your own—the achievements, the struggles, all the experiences that have made you what you are. How might those attributes help you make the jump to a nonprofit job?

Rather than diving directly into that question, I want to start by sharing seven true stories of successful transitions, leaders who rose through various for-profit roles and landed in diverse nonprofit settings. I'll let these leaders speak for themselves to inform your own process.

Spotlight

ALFREDO MARTEL: Totally Prepared to Make the Jump

Alfredo Martel is the new President and CEO of Meda (Metropolitan Economic Development Association) in Minneapolis. A few minutes with Alfredo is all it takes to catch his excitement for his work. He feels absolutely called to leading an organization with a mission of supporting minority-owned businesses. Alfredo comes to Meda following a highly successful corporate career in marketing and general management at companies like Yum! Brands (KFC, Pizza Hut, Taco Bell) and Caribou Coffee.

While this is Alfredo's first permanent job at a nonprofit, he isn't entirely new to the sector. Alfredo comes to Meda from the Walker Art Center, where he was Interim Chief of Marketing and Strategic Communications. Full disclosure: I presented the opportunity at Meda to Alfredo. I knew Alfredo was well-prepared and on-point. His interim experience had given him language, connections, and understanding as a nonprofit practitioner so his transition appeared seamless.

Q: How did you make your move into the nonprofit sector?

I was an active board member at a nonprofit called The Brand Lab, which prepares students for careers in marketing and advertising. I was deeply involved and brought The Brand Lab into Caribou Coffee for volunteer engagements and other projects.

Simultaneously, I was a board member at the Walker Art Center during a period of major change and executive transition. During it all, the board chair asked me to step into an interim position as head of marketing and communications. It was incredibly eye-opening for me to move from the board level, where we were focused on governance, to the staff level, where our job was execution. I learned a ton.

Q: What was the most important thing you gained in your interim role?

As a senior staff member, I had to change from board lens to functional lens. I saw firsthand how much work, creativity, and tenacity is required to get things done in the sector.

Q: You've also worked with an executive coach. Was that helpful?

Yes! Very impactful. I had a coach years ago at Bristol Myers, and I took the opportunity to be coached seriously. My coach said I still had a lot to learn. What a gift! I was grateful.

Later, coaching helped me realize what I love to do. I realized that I *loved* my work at the Walker. I was happiest building a team around a mission.

Q: How has your corporate background transferred to your nonprofit role?

Meda is a nonprofit focused on business, so the mission is friendly to my background. When I meet with boards and clients, we speak the same language. My background in franchising means I can talk about growth, impact, and scale—and that resonates at Meda. It was crucial to have that connection.

Q: What advice do you have for people who would love to follow your example?

Be yourself. Don't try too hard. Be calm. At first, I was focused on hearing what I lacked so I could address it. I was coached to shift my attention to be strengths-focused.

Be prepared. I thoroughly read Meda's 990 financial reports and came prepared to discuss them.

Have a point of view. Don't avoid discussions for fear of being wrong. The hiring executives didn't care if my perspectives were right or wrong. They valued hearing my thought process.

Q: Anything else?

People ask me a lot how I made the jump. For me, it all started with the self-reflection, figuring out what does and doesn't work for me as a person. Finding the right space is critical. And if the journey toward nonprofit doesn't seem to be working, get coaching!

Q: Was this the right choice?

Yes! I was ready. I find the wholistic sense of nonprofit to be refreshing. Recently I was at a foundation event where nonprofit leaders from around the country were networking and meeting. I caught myself; there was no "careering." I realized that none of us are competing here! Done well, it's all about collaboration.

Spotlight

DEB BROBERG: Follow Your Profession

I met Deb three years ago when she was first considering a move to nonprofit. She's impressive, with a background including senior human resources leadership roles at Wells Fargo and Northwest Airlines. Fast forward: Deb is now Executive Director of RealTime Talent, a Minnesota nonprofit organization serving hiring organizations in finding and recruiting talent. This public-private collaborative closes the gap of aligning potential talent with organizations struggling to find it.

Q: How did you get into the nonprofit sector?

I left Wells Fargo in 2016 and spent 12 months networking to learn more about the nonprofit sector. After that discovery process, I offered my human resources services on a pro bono basis to three large nonprofits. Each organization had a unique mission and a fair bit of complexity. One project led to a request to engage me in a longer-term consulting role.

Then I crossed paths with the board chair at RealTime Talent. The group's work was born out of a major regional think tank and research around regional staffing forecasts—including the need to think more creatively about how to close hiring gaps with available talent, particularly those from underserved communities.

This mission resonated with me and I decided to apply. I met several board members during a robust hiring process and was offered the position.

Q: I like how you combined tons of networking with pro bono and paid assignments. You worked across the nonprofit sector.

Yes. I learned it was important to keep an open mind. You can't leave any stone unturned. The plan will emerge, and it will reveal itself.

Q: What about your background did the RealTime Talent board find most compelling?

During my search process, I had connected with the City of Minneapolis and evaluated the city's use of federal dollars. I received feedback from RealTime Talent that I might be a strong candidate because of my exposure to federal funding. They also appreciated my background in a variety of organizational cultures, and my comfort with finance and budgeting.

And I heard consistently that the key to this role is relationship building.

Q: What does relationship building look like in the context of RealTime Talent?

Relationship building looks like finding common ground. Listening is a big part. Good relationships are long-term, and that requires patience and persistence. And we need to work with and through others. As I navigate between pools of potential candidates and organizations with job openings, I don't often have positional power. Personal power is a must.

Q: Is your role in the nonprofit sector what you expected?

Overall, yes. But what I didn't realize was the difficulty of getting buy-in "across stakeholders." I've been able to bring about funding shifts that serve us well. But we'll need to innovate even further. Sometimes private sector players oversimplify the nonprofit space. It's far more complicated than they know.

Q: What do you wish you had known before joining the nonprofit sector?

Nonprofit organizations often have complex, multifaceted funding streams. For this role, I wish I had understood the grant cycle and the complexity of managing so many sub-categories within the grants area. I wasted a lot of time figuring that out.

Q: Final words?

A job in the nonprofit sector isn't for everyone. Passion isn't enough. People say, "I can't believe you actually made the shift. I want to do that!" So I say, "You better start making different choices now." You need to make choices about lifestyle and preparation so you can be in a position to do this.

And allow yourself time. There's no way I would ever tell someone they can successfully jump to the nonprofit sector in 12 months. It simply takes longer.

Q: Was this the right choice?

Yes, I feel good about my work. But there are always new challenges. I didn't know what I didn't know. The learning curve is to be open because until you can get "in the chair" in a meaningful way, you really don't know. And that's okay.

Spotlight

DON NESS: Follow Your Love of Place

Don Ness is the Executive Director of the Ordean Foundation in Duluth, Minnesota, a philanthropic organization supporting organizations in the Duluth area. Prior to becoming the leader at Ordean Foundation, Don had a prominent career in public service. He was elected Mayor of Duluth at age 33, the youngest mayor to lead that city. He ran unopposed for a second term and achieved an amazing 89 percent approval rating while in office. Don is also the author of *Hillsider: Snapshots of a Curious Political Journey.*

Q: Wow. What a background. Where did your drive to serve the Duluth region come from?

My parents. My father was the pastor of a local church and later a chaplain. My mother worked in social services. I guess I'm grounded in my parents' values. In both politics and social services, you're connecting people's talents with providing services.

Q: How did you successfully "make the jump" after such a successful political career?

I learned that political games don't work. And that the trappings of political life—attention, recognition, making decisions—can become addictive. For me, it was important to separate the trappings as part of the job versus part of who I am.

Q: What about your role in philanthropy? Can you draw any parallels with public service?

Yes. Whether I'm working at city hall or in a nonprofit, the community is still the canvass. At Ordean Foundation, I use my knowledge of the community to examine it through a new lens. I step out of seeing problems as a government issue and look for new ways to approach them.

Q: What about size of organization? You went from a city government to a foundation with far fewer staff.

The most challenging part of that is seeing impact differently. As Mayor, I didn't have to go out and talk about the work I was doing because it was self-evident. In a nonprofit with a specialized mission, I need to think about impact and messaging quite differently. For me, philanthropy has been the right fit as we can address entrenched problems in the community.

Q: Advice for others?

You'll need to see impact differently. As Mayor, I was in the room where big decisions were made. We had big levers to solve problems. Perhaps you're an executive with a similar experience. I find value when we see suffering alleviated and people's lives improved.

Spotlight

JOHN GORDON: Follow Your Career Direction

After a 35-plus year career as a partner at a major law firm, John Gordon retired—but didn't slow down. He taught at the university level and consulted. And he continued his long-time involvement with the American Civil Liberties Union (ACLU) of Minnesota. When the ACLU needed an interim executive director for several months, John stepped in. Voila! John loved it! The organization was searching for a new Executive Director. John knew it was right for him. He threw his hat in the ring and was awarded the role.

Q: You have a great story—your move to the ACLU.

I was happy teaching and doing mediation. But I felt called to do more.

Q: Did the organization's board question your motivation?

I answered that question right away. "Who wouldn't want this job?" I said. The organization was sound. It has a mission to improve lives, especially the most marginalized. We all enjoy the benefits of democracy. My interest was clear.

We did have to discuss the fact that I'd never run an organization like this. My previous board experience was hugely valuable. I understood the nonprofit sector at a strategic level. My experience on high-functioning boards showed me how it all comes together when done well.

Q: What about the fundraising that comes with your leadership role? Were you prepared to do that?

My board experiences prepared me. And I've never been uncomfortable asking for money. I needed to learn specific tactics and systems, but over the years I've become comfortable reaching out to the community to generate support.

Q: What do you wish you had known before joining the nonprofit sector?

Nonprofit organizations are more oriented to process. There is more transparency, more inclusion, more voices. Getting good results is nice, but not sufficient. The way the results are achieved also matter.

Q: Advice for others seeking to move into nonprofit?

Be picky. You'll know it when you see it.

Understand the similarities and differences between corporate and nonprofit. Not everything is transferable. Be comfortable with both.

Spotlight

KATHLEEN ANNETTE, MD: Follow Your Leadership

Dr. Kathleen Annette is the first Ojibwe woman to become a medical doctor. Much of her career was spent in leadership positions in the United States Indian Health Service, culminating in a role as Acting Deputy of

Field Operations, a job that oversaw operations in all 50 states. In 2011, Dr. Annette was named CEO at the Blandin Foundation, a nationally known philanthropic organization serving rural communities throughout Minnesota.

Q: You transitioned successfully from health care administration to philanthropy.
After just a few years of practicing as a physician, I moved into leadership and have held leadership roles ever since.

Q: What has helped you be successful?
What I know is that leaders at all levels and all organizations have a common objective. First, the leader must get a feel for the culture. Then the leader must decide "Is this the right culture to accomplish the mission?" Every two years we do a "rural pulse" survey. In the past, things like education and economy have been at the top of the list. Now, health care is at the top.

To be successful, we must listen to the communities we serve. I brought an orientation toward listening from my time at Indian Health Service. We *stand with* communities—we don't *do for* communities. They would not want to be *done for*.

Q: What surprised you most about moving from health care into a foundation?
Accountability is very different. In health care, accountability is key. Literally, or people die. In philanthropy, we have accountability, but the work isn't as crisis-oriented. We figure things out absent the extreme pressures. It has been a joy to have the luxury of time.

Q: You had history with the Blandin Foundation, having been a board member some years before becoming CEO.
Yes. But the board had a totally different composition when I was a member. As a woman and a person of color, I was conscious of when I spoke at meetings or even *if* I spoke. The Foundation has always had a highly functional

board, but there's been an evolution in the last several years to be a fully engaged and diverse board. We work hard to accommodate diverse views.

Q: Many rural nonprofit organizations seek leaders. Advice for others seeking to move into nonprofits in a rural setting?
People tend to paint rural communities with one brush. Each community has different strengths and challenges, and their emphasis is different. Rural residents love living rural. Themes from these communities are around commitment to family, nature, and neighbors. Rural communities are changing and that's why we're here.

Spotlight

JODY HORNER: Being Open to a Call
Jody Horner is president of Midland University in Fremont, Nebraska. Her prior role was as president of Cargill Meat Solutions and Cargill Case Ready, where she was responsible for a multi-billion-dollar corporation with more than 3,000 employees supplying some of the world's largest retailers. Before taking over Cargill Meat Solutions and Cargill Case Ready, she served as president of one of the world's largest food, industrial, and agricultural salt enterprises.

Q: How did you get into the nonprofit sector?
I didn't find nonprofit—it found me! I still remember the day I turned 50. My youngest son was getting ready to go to college, and we were becoming empty nesters. I was still working at Cargill, 30 years after I started. The transitions made me think about doing something different. I began to ponder "What should I do next?" I considered several options and left myself open to many.

I had been serving on the board of my alma mater, St. Olaf College, when a recruiter called to invite me to consider an opportunity as president of a small university. This was a role that I hadn't yet considered but I decided to learn more. Several conversations later—over time—I felt "called" to the position.

The Midland University board was seeking a businessperson with a passion for education. As it is a Lutheran institution, my own faith tradition as a Lutheran was important as well.

Q: How important was your board experience at an academic institution?
My board experience at St. Olaf was extremely important. I'm not sure I'd have been ready for this role without it. My other board experience, such as at Big Brothers Big Sisters, was also valuable.

Q: Which leadership characteristic has been most important in your new role?
Humility. I believe you must have the courage to be humble. The work is about the mission and a leader needs to remember "It's not about me." I've found that faculty and staff want authenticity. They can see through false presentation. Don't sell yourself short but let go of arrogance. Moving toward the mission with humility is number one.

Q: What advice do you have for other leaders new to their jobs in the nonprofit sector?
Know your "why." This transition is a big one for you and your family. If you're thinking about "giving back," realize there are lots of ways to give back. What specifically do you want to do and why? I found my why.

Realize you will work extremely hard. The learning curve is steep. I've never worked so hard in my life.

You still need to achieve results—and you might have to achieve results with few resources. For example, in corporate life, there are usually resources to develop staff through conferences and seminars. I still need to develop staff now, but without the resources. Nonprofit leaders must be more creative.

Q: Final words?
I've never been happier in my career! I loved my corporate career. Indeed, it led me to this role. I'm where I am supposed to be. This position pulls together my passion for higher education, my faith, my P&L background, and my commitment to service.

Spotlight

MORRIS GOODWIN, JR.:
Board Leadership to Sector Leadership

Morris Goodwin is one of the most highly regarded nonprofit leaders I know. With an MBA from Stanford University and roles in executive finance and treasury, he transferred to the nonprofit sector several years ago after an impressive corporate career as Vice President and Treasurer at American Express Financial Advisors and Deluxe Corporation. A music aficionado, Morris is currently the Senior Vice President and Chief Financial Officer at American Public Media Group.

Q: How did you get into the nonprofit sector?

As a corporate executive at American Express Financial Advisors, I was encouraged to become active on boards and serve the nonprofit community. I joined several boards—and loved it.

I was later presented with the chance to join Wilder Foundation, a large and complex nonprofit. I connected with the work. It was "more pull than push" for me.

Q: What about the work of Wilder Foundation did you find compelling?

Wilder was doing "soul work." That resonated with me. They were doing what I experienced growing up. It's how we took care of each other.

Q: Was your faith a component in your decision to join a nonprofit organization?

Absolutely. I was just starting deaconate training in the Episcopal faith tradition. There was a spirit-felt passion about Wilder's work. It wasn't "religious" but rather spirit-enhancing, spirit-inducing. I found I could meld my faith with my work and not make apologies for it.

Q: How important were your nonprofit board experiences?

Immensely important. I believe that you have to be naturalized—socialized—into the nonprofit milieu before coming into a nonprofit organization.

Just like you had to know something to get the jobs you've had, you'll need to know the issues, strategies, and governance relevant to the nonprofit sector. Not that it's foreign, but it isn't the same.

Board service gave me that. I had relationships, knowledge, and credibility before I started.

My board experiences consisted of stimulating, important, strategic interactions. I had a good sense of the sector, so I knew what I was getting into.

Q: So your first nonprofit role was what you expected?

Yes, mostly.

Q: What would have been helpful to know before joining the nonprofit sector?

Three elements dogged me at first.

The first was *contextual.* I needed to understand and appreciate differences—geographic location, race and ethnicity, faith, among other factors. These were elemental in how people connected and reacted to each other.

The second was *facing the reality of the work,* including trauma-informed health care services. I did not know how extensive the disparities are. I had to steel myself every day to face issues I'd not had to face before.

Finally, *regulations.* I'd been around regulatory complexity and oversight in corporations. Nonprofits, by comparison, can be a byzantine stranglehold of regulations. There are much wider degrees of freedom in corporate. And in corporate, you're not risking your very soul and belief system the way you do in nonprofit. If you're involved in the regulatory side of an organization, realize it might be something you know nothing about. It's a different world than where you came from.

Success!

As a group, these talented individuals stand out for their expertise and accomplishments. They all have unique stories and contributions to their organizations and sectors. Still, there are themes that run through the narratives:

- All leaders shared a conscious goal to live **a purpose-driven life** and to have that purpose extend into the workplace.

- Each story is full of **intention.** These leaders didn't get to their desired next position by happenstance. They had a formal thought process and action process that guided their journey.

- Most leaders experienced surprises and several landed in roles not on their radar at the start. However, all their career transitions were powered by **commitment** to reach the right endpoint.

How about you? What points of their stories resonate with your own experience? Are you ready for that intentional journey?

Let me help you think that through.

CHAPTER THREE

The Awakening

More than a few callers to my open line seem to think everything about the nonprofit sector is easy.

As in easy to enter. Easy to transfer pretty much any background to any nonprofit role. And an easier, more enjoyable work experience once settled in. So what's not to like? Callers envision a lighter load, lower expectations, shorter hours, less pressure. Lastly, they assume any discrepancies in background or expectations will be magically overcome by passion—or even a passing interest—in the organization's mission.

Is that your impulse?

No?

Are you certain?

Before we go further, this is the moment I encourage you to stop. Get real. Dig deep. Commit to complete honesty with yourself.

**I invite you to double check whether
you genuinely want to work in the nonprofit sector.**

Most business leaders face significant, unanticipated challenges at non-profits. When they do, their background is sometimes the reason. It is often the case their past success in another sector turns out to be more of a liability than an asset. They struggle with their new role, with their new life, and even with the decision that led them to a nonprofit in the first place.

Consider Jacques.

Jacques joined the board of KidsKare three years ago, soon after he and his wife became empty nesters when their youngest left for college. The couple had always been concerned about the cost of high-quality child-care. They felt fortunate to be able to afford care, which allowed each to pursue demanding careers in sales.

Jacques had first connected with KidsKare when he was invited to a fund-raising luncheon by a neighbor whose firm performed the group's annual audits. He hadn't heard of KidsKare, and he was intrigued to learn the organization raised money for scholarships so qualifying parents could enroll their children in solid childcare near their home or office. KidsKare also assisted childcare providers by sharing best practices. Jacques gladly contributed to KidsKare.

A few months later, Jacques' neighbor asked if he wanted to get more involved with the organization, alerting him to an open board spot.

After meeting the KidsKare Executive Director and other board members, Jacques accepted an invitation to join the board, whose members impressed him as talented and committed community leaders.

Jacques went deeper when he joined the Governance Committee. With only 18 staff members, they managed to accomplish much with few resources.

Then, a year ago, the Executive Director unexpectedly resigned to care for a partner with health issues. To ease the transition, the Executive Director gave a three-month notice and offered to assist in hiring her successor.

The board was unsure what to do next, but Jacques was impressed with the board chair's actions as she partnered with the Executive Director, meeting with staff as a group and individually to explain upcoming changes. It became clear that none of the current employees was interested in applying for the Executive Director position.

To save money, the board decided to recruit a new Executive Director on their own. They created a job description using existing information and fresh input from the outgoing Executive Director, and posted it on area job websites.

A small group of board members, including one with a background in human resources, formed a committee to review applications and conduct interviews.

Jacques and other board members received frequent updates during months of ongoing recruiting. A handful of candidates were interviewed, but the committee determined none met KidsKare's current needs. The job required someone who could manage staff, interact with external stakeholders, collaborate with the board, and inspire passion in the community about access to quality childcare. Fitting candidates weren't coming forward.

At one point, Jacques was recounting the situation to his wife. "We're just not finding the right person," he told her. She hesitated. Then, she suggested, "Why don't you apply?"

Jacques thought about it. And thought. And thought some more. He was passionate about KidsKare and its mission. He knew many of the staff.

He worked well with the board. And wasn't fundraising really no different than sales?

A couple months passed before Jacques decided to approach the board chair about his interest in the role. By that time, he and his wife had had several conversations about the possibility. Were Jacques to accept the position, he would take a significant pay cut. But they had done well and managed their money well, so they could make this work.

The board chair was surprised and relieved to learn of Jacques' interest in the Executive Director position. Things moved quickly. Jacques talked to a group of board members assembled as a hiring committee about how he felt his sales and sales management career would transfer well to running a nonprofit. The committee gave their approval and encouraged Jacques to talk to the outgoing Executive Director as a final step.

The conversation with the Executive Director gave Jacques a clearer sense of upcoming projects, current issues of the organization, and red flags with funding streams. The outgoing leader was gracious but seemed somewhat less positive about Jacques succeeding her than board members were.

A few weeks later, the Executive Director enjoyed a well-attended celebration of her many years with the organization. Looking on, Jacques heard story after story about how KidsKare had impacted families in the community. He was happy to be involved with such a meaningful organization.

For his part, Jacques was feted by his fellow sales executives as he left for the nonprofit sector. His colleagues wished him well and encouraged him to stay in touch.

As Jacques began at KidsKare, a nice announcement went out to organizational partners and donors, with a small mention in the local newspaper. Jacques was on his way in a new career.

Fast forward six months.

Jacques is the not-so-new Executive Director. It's almost 9 p.m. and he's still at the office. As he prepares for an upcoming board meeting, Jacques is reflecting on the past few months. He feels pensive. Leading KidsKare hasn't been easy.

Jacques wishes he had known then what he knows now. But if he had, would he have taken the job?

He ticks off some of the facets of the role that he didn't expect:

- **The nonprofit sector—childcare in particular—is as nuanced as any corporate sector.** Despite being on the board, Jacques lacked vocabulary and content well-known by staff and partners at KidsKare. The complexity of grants and contracts were beyond anything he had experienced so far in his career.

- **Fundraising and sales are decidedly NOT the same thing.** The Executive Director at KidsKare sets fundraising strategy and messaging, carries a portfolio of major donors, and is held accountable to a fundraising target. The board has been understanding thus far, but Jacques is way behind on his fundraising goals and in no position to guide the fundraising team.

- The KidsKare **culture** is entirely different from his former company. It's hard to explain, but he doesn't fit. He still feels like an outsider. Jacques recognizes management is practiced differently here, but he doesn't know what to change.

- Jacques still likes the **board members**, but relationships have changed. Before, Jacques asked the questions. Now, he's expected to have all the answers. He's no longer part of the team and misses the old camaraderie.

- No one told Jacques how important it would be for him to **cultivate relationships** across the sector and with government, philanthropic, and corporate funders as well as elected officials. He had a list of people to meet, but as soon as he checked one off, three more popped up. How would he juggle it all?

- **The financials.** Yikes. For a small organization, money was complicated. It didn't help that the organization couldn't afford up-to-date accounting software, making financial reports even more difficult to decipher. Jacques was a sales pro, after all, not a numbers guy. As a board member, he glanced at financials without digging in. He didn't have to, because others were happy to get into the weeds. Now those folks are looking to him!

He could go on. Jacques recalled telling the interview committee that his corporate sales background would enable him to bring "best practices" to KidsKare. Well, that hadn't worked out. He was barely keeping his head above water, much less instituting best practices.

More hours. Added stress. Less sense of accomplishment.

Twice the board chair had called him to check in. The chair noted that critical fundraising objectives weren't being met, and other organizational goals were lagging. She offered to help Jacques, suggesting he might benefit from a coach—one from the nonprofit sector. Jacques appreciated the offer but was hoping to make it alone.

Now, he wasn't so sure.

Are *You* Up to the Challenge?

In any sector, a new job is a new job. Even if you stay in the same type of job in the same type of organization, you expect challenges and a learning curve. If the nonprofit sector is new to you, double the learning curve. If the job is a new type of job, triple the challenge.

Are you up for it?

And by the way—can I talk you out of this?

What? Why would I want to talk you out of doing something as noble as seeking to move into the nonprofit sector?

Noble as it may sound, a move to the nonprofit sector brings risk. You might indeed be up for the challenge, but I want you to know all the facts so you can make an informed decision.

For this transition to be successful, a multitude of things need to be in place. The first is that your motivation to join the nonprofit sector is sincere.

"Of course!" you think. "What other motivation could I possibly have?"

Well, several possible motivations that might initially drive a person toward the nonprofit sector but will not sustain. Here are a few:

- *I need a job.* I want to work in the nonprofit sector because I'm not finding work in the corporate sector.

- *I'm frustrated.* I'm interested in the nonprofit sector because I've had so many interviews for jobs at companies and I'm just not getting any offers.

- *I'm done with business.* I don't like how I was treated. Maybe it will be better in nonprofit.

- *I need a change.* Who knows? Maybe the nonprofit sector will be refreshingly different.

The list goes on:

- *I've made enough money.* I'm financially comfortable. It's time for me to give back.

- *Life will be easier in the nonprofit sector.* The work won't require as much of me.

- *I don't want to work as hard anymore.* My hours will be shorter in the nonprofit sector.

And then there's:

- *I'm sure to impress the nonprofit sector.* I'll be welcomed with open arms and (finally) appreciated.

- *My friends and relatives will be impressed.* They'll respect my "sacrifice."

- *This will be in line with my religious or spiritual beliefs.* I've felt empty not fully living out my purpose.

Where do you recognize yourself in those comments—or not?

Along with being certain of your motivations, getting clear on nonprofit realities is also essential. As I work with corporate leaders seeking a nonprofit role, I feel compelled to raise these potential concerns from the start. So why wouldn't you want to pursue a job in the nonprofit sector?

Time

It might take you a long while to get a job in the nonprofit sector—most likely, much longer than to find a job at a for-profit organization. If you're a skilled manufacturing manager, for example, you could likely get a job in a similar role in the manufacturing sector far more quickly than you could land a role in a nonprofit organization.

Consider: Are you okay if it takes twice as long to move to a nonprofit rather than stay in your current sector? How about three times as long? Or if the transition takes years rather than months? Do you have financial resources to be without work while you look?

Depending upon your precise background, the time to secure a role in the nonprofit sector will vary, of course. But it will take longer.

Effort

Seeking a job in a new sector always takes extra time. That means extra work. Why? It's easier to find a job similar to the work you currently do, because your skills and experience are a more obvious fit to the new opportunity. It's simply harder to move to a new sector where you, by necessity, must convince others your skills will transfer—despite what you've already accomplished in your career.

You'll have to work more diligently to discover and pursue opportunities in the nonprofit sector. You might lack contacts to call on. You may not know exactly where to look for appropriate postings.

Because your background may not be as related to the jobs you're examining in the nonprofit sector, you may have to compete for more of them, knowing you won't get through as frequently. You'll have to meet with twice as many people and send in twice as many applications. You'll need dogged determination to track and follow up on your activities. Some people don't want the realities of a "high effort" job search. It won't be easy.

Consider: Will being turned down give you energy to learn more for the next time—or will it beat you down? Will you get frustrated and give up?

Of course, there are exceptions to both the investment of time and effort outlined above. Larger nonprofits that rely more on earned revenue than donated revenue have many functions that are common in the corporate sector—sales, marketing, accounting, human resources, information technology, etc. And many of them even feel more corporate than nonprofit. Many large health care organizations, for instance, are nonprofits.

Another exception is 501(c)(6) nonprofits—member associations focusing on professions or trades. Your years in a law firm may position you for a leadership role in a bar association, albeit most likely at a lower salary, which we discuss below. Your career with a radio station might prepare you well to lead a broadcasting association.

But let's assume your soul searching has moved you more toward smaller nonprofit organizations that rely on a mix of earned and donated revenue, perhaps even skewing more heavily toward the latter.

Pay

In almost every case, a comparable job at a nonprofit organization will pay less than its counterpart job in the for-profit sector.

> *Consider: Are you okay taking a cut in pay? Further, are you also okay if the benefits package is less comprehensive?*

Be aware that no matter how fantastic you are, nonprofit organizations won't break the bank or spring for fat bonuses to get you on board. Fairness is the thing. If you're awarded a position, you'll get an offer comparable to others in the organization who perform the same function. I had one nonprofit client whose practice was to pay the Executive Director no greater than three times the pay of the lowest paid staff member. Try and find that in the for-profit sector.

Most likely, you'll also be provided with a lesser set of benefits, and you'll need to contribute more. Again, don't expect an offer with perquisites different from others on staff. It is what it is. Be absolutely sure you're comfortable with the financial factors of the jobs you're targeting.

Learning Curve

Moving into a new sector means needing to learn a ton. New concepts. New phrases. New organizations, services, and leaders. The whole thing. In much of this process, you'll be a student, not an expert.

Certainly, you can start learning and preparing now. There are efficient ways to gain knowledge about the nonprofit sector, such as seminars and online courses. But it could be a lot of effort. And it will only be the beginning.

> *Consider: Are you okay taking on the role of learner? Will you be good if others don't immediately regard you as an expert? Do you have the time, perseverance, and humility to remain a lifelong learner in your new role?*

As you consider various positions, you'll be best served by long conversations with corporate leaders who have made similar moves—some recently, some long ago. They can give you an insider perspective on the transition experience. They know what it really takes.

Still Interested?

Okay. Let's say you've looked in the mirror and dug deep into your motivations. You have clarity that your interest in the nonprofit sector is sincere. Despite the challenges of time, effort, pay, and learning, you believe the nonprofit sector is right for you and want to move ahead.

You might think I'm making it sound as if nonprofits don't want you.

That's not exactly what I'm trying to communicate.

Nonprofit organizations seek great people who can help them further their mission. They seek partners and associates, fundraisers, and program leaders. They don't know you specifically, but like all organizational sectors, nonprofits need great people to do great work. The must-answer questions are these:

Are you the right great person for a role?

And in what type of organization will you do best?

And, finally, what would it take to get there?

CHAPTER 4

What Nonprofits Want

The most common question I'm asked by businesspeople contemplating a move to the nonprofit sector—by far—is this:

What are THEY looking for?

I get it. You want a sense of whether your background and experiences would match jobs in the nonprofit sector. You don't want to apply without knowing you're on the right track. Why go down a path that simply won't lead to an offer?

That's fine. But there's a problem. It's the word *they*.

**Asking a question like "What are *they* looking for?"
about the nonprofit sector is like inquiring,
"What do for-profit organizations look for?"**

It's absurdly broad. Do you mean jobs in manufacturing? Banking? Retail? What *they* want in each sector would be worlds apart. And what type of job? Head of human resources? Administrative assistant? Supply chain manager?

"What are *they* looking for?" is equally strange in the nonprofit world. *They* probably want a host of things, but it all depends upon the organization and role. What *they* need in a new head of the local Chamber of Commerce is totally different from what *they* need to lead operations at an animal shelter. And a fundraiser for a parochial grade school? That's yet another set of boxes to check.

Drop that question when you talk with people in the nonprofit world. It won't yield valuable information. Rather, it might give the impression you're uninformed about the sector or haven't done your homework. It may even imply you think all jobs in all nonprofit organizations are looking for the same thing. Do you really mean that?

Of course not!

What Nonprofits *Don't* Want

I don't want to entirely dismiss the "What are they looking for?" question. Set it aside for a moment and turn it around: "What are they *not* looking for?" That's far easier to answer, especially in the context of an individual seeking to pivot to a nonprofit.

- **Nonprofits are *not* looking for someone near the end of a career who views nonprofits as a rest stop before retirement.** It's repellent to those who have dedicated their lives to a cause when someone views their organization as a short-term gig or offramp.

- **Nonprofits are *not* looking for someone who has made their name elsewhere and suddenly wants to "give back."** Give back to what? To whom? Although many nonprofits are charitable organizations, your newfound availability doesn't seem as charitable to them as it does to you. There are many more sincere ways to self-actualize than drawing a paycheck from a nonprofit. They might prefer you give back with your checkbook, for example, rather than via your job application.

- **Nonprofits are *not* looking for someone looking to bring the discipline of for-profit business to their organization.** Many would argue their nonprofit businesses are significantly more disciplined than most for-profit businesses. They have to be. Their margins are generally much tighter. And remember that mission statement discussion? They *must* prove to funders they are achieving their mission. How many for-profits do that?

- **Nonprofits are *not* looking for someone with passion without commensurate skills and experience.** Doesn't your interest in getting into a nonprofit count for something? Sure! Interest is outstanding. But most applicants for most jobs are energized about the role they've applied for, right? Interest won't set you apart from other candidates.

Nonprofits aren't a training ground, a scenic overlook, or a recharging station—anymore than any other organization.

What Nonprofits Do Want

Let's come back to the original question: "What are they looking for?"

Narrow it down to a segment of the nonprofit world—and a specific organization—and an identifiable role—and the question starts to make sense.

Like most organizations, nonprofits are populated with good people trying their best. Those staff have roles and responsibilities and need to hire others around them to further the objectives and achieve the mission. What they want are candidates who bring the skills, experience, and characteristics necessary for a particular job.

They seek qualified candidates. Like everyone else. That's it.

If you've hired staff, you've done it with an eye toward the work that needs to be done and the communication and leadership style and characteristics that will facilitate the process. You probably have honed a job description that lays out must-have and nice-to-have qualifications. You can flex to a point, but you mostly zero in on the must-haves.

Nonprofits want the same thing any organization does— proven (or at least related) skills to do the job.

With that in mind, I want to point out there are indeed skills and experience valued by nearly all nonprofits.

Revenue Generation

Like for-profit businesses, nonprofits need revenue to remain operating and making an impact. Revenue generally falls into two broad categories: earned revenue and contributed revenue.

- **Earned revenue** is the result of program-generated revenue, fee for service revenue, sales revenue, dues revenue, contract revenue, etc.

- **Contributed revenue** typically comes in the form of individual donations, corporate donations (financial and in-kind), and foundation grants.

In addition, some nonprofit organizations rely on government contracts as important revenue streams. These contracts can be federal, state, or county level agreements. They can be extremely complex.

- If you're looking at a role where **government contracts** make up a large part of the organization's revenue—often fee for service revenue—you'll be expected to have experience overseeing those types of financial agreements.

- If you're seeking a position at the top of a charitable nonprofit, significant background in **fundraising**—contributed revenue—will be valued, if not required. Many nonprofit organizations rely on contributed revenue as an important revenue stream; in some cases, it is the only revenue stream.

If fundraising is listed as a primary qualification for a job, be aware proof of direct experience raising money will likely be a key requirement. Service on a giving committee is great, but it doesn't count as full fundraising experience. Assisting with a gala is also good. But again, it's not truly fundraising. Even if there is a Director of Fund Development on staff, the organization's top executive is always involved in major fundraising work.

Be prepared to talk about how many dollars you've personally raised. Have you approached major and principal donors? Led an annual campaign? Headed a capital campaign? Written and managed grants? What types? Have you been involved in planned giving?

Fundraising is a complex field that takes many years to master. And this is an unforeseen difficulty for most corporate folks, who don't have requisite fundraising background to enter many nonprofit leadership jobs. If you've acquired fundraising experience over the years, good for you. It will be extraordinarily helpful to you now.

External/Government Relations

Nonprofit organizations often build connections to a wide variety of stakeholders including institutional funders, individual donors, elected officials, and wider community groups. There's frequently a need for senior nonprofit executives to represent the organization's mission in these circles. Those efforts can range from public speaking to large groups to lobbying elected officials on policy issues. The top leader at a nonprofit must be prepared to be the face and voice of the organization during business and non-business hours.

Thought Leadership

The nonprofit sector is intensely competitive. There are battles for government contracts, foundation grants, and individual donor dollars earmarked for philanthropy. Each funder wants to give to organizations that can prove they make a difference.

Offering a fully-stocked food shelf to a community, for example, doesn't cut it anymore. What else is that food shelf doing to actually end hunger or increase nutrition where it operates? Professional associations can no longer count on reflexive membership renewals. What are those associations doing to remain relevant when its members can get free education online and can network with each other on LinkedIn?

Diversity, Equity, and Inclusion

Leaders in the nonprofit sector are expected to have a strong commitment to diversity, equity, and inclusion (DEI). While this imperative has become increasingly important for businesses, it has long been bedrock for most nonprofits.

Most nonprofit organizations seek to live out diversity, equity, and inclusion in their work. They seek staff members committed to its practice. They may rightfully want an executive with lived experience in the community being served. And they often seek staff members with practical involvement in creating and implementing DEI initiatives. Expect targeted questions about your background with DEI, and you will want to be able to illustrate your answers with sophisticated experience in this area.

Board Experience

If you're seeking a senior executive position at a nonprofit, you will likely be asked about your experience working with boards. The executive director or president of a nonprofit reports directly to a board of directors.

Direct reports to the top leader will probably attend and report at board meetings and staff board committees.

Have you served on nonprofit or for-profit boards? Presented to boards? Prepared materials for others to present? Supported a board committee? Any board experience is valuable and will make you a more suitable candidate for senior roles at a nonprofit.

Related Experience in Nonprofits

Here's another place where I must be honest. This point lies at the intersection of "nonprofits are easy" and "My skills will transfer. Isn't that obvious?" Many callers to my open line underestimate the competition they will face in their attempt to make the jump to a nonprofit job. As you have been building your business career, many in the nonprofit world have been gaining hard-fought experience that prepares them for greater leadership.

The Homegrown Competition

As you evaluate your own ability to enter the nonprofit sector, consider the resumes of leaders who have worked their way up through that system.

The following are composite descriptions of real people. They show resumes of nonprofit leaders with just enough details altered to protect confidentiality.

Jorge Carillo

Jorge is Vice President of Programs for a mid-sized nonprofit. He began his career doing direct service work serving people with cognitive disabilities, where he carried a caseload of clients with special needs and gifts. Jorge earned a master's degree in social work, leaving him with large student debt. While his job barely paid above minimum wage, Jorge took pride and joy in his work, becoming a champion for his clients and a supporter and ally of their families. When the organization was understaffed, Jorge volunteered to assist on overnight shifts. His work was demanding and the hours long.

After three years, Jorge was promoted to Manager of Client Services, earning a small pay raise and the chance to gain supervisory skills. Without funds for management training, Jorge learned on the job and used days off to meet with friends and mentors for advice.

Two years later, Jorge spotted an opening for a Director of Client Support Programs at a larger nonprofit serving a broader geographic area. He applied for the position and was hired. For the next 10 years, Jorge tackled the challenges of managing staff at a dozen locations. The group provided services 24/7, meaning Jorge had to be accessible day or night. Jorge knew his pay equaled a fraction of what his friends earned at for-profits in similar management positions. But the work was meaningful to Jorge and that mattered most.

Along the way, Jorge managed to pay off his student debt. A capital campaign at his organization put him in front of donors and funders as part of a fundraising team. Jorge found creative ways to continue his own education through grant-funded programs and seminars, and a pilot program offering an executive roundtable experience for nonprofit leaders. As the years went on, Jorge assumed responsibility for clinical quality and program development. A recent newspaper article named him one of the state's Most Valued Leaders in the nonprofit sector.

Jorge has earned several certifications in the disability and mental health services fields. He's on the board of the regional Access to Services Council and was named a fellow at the local college's human services degree program. The latter allows him to participate in panels and lectures to train the next generation of nonprofit professionals. He's well-known as a gracious leader, a developer of people, and a strategic thinker.

Jorge has recently been contacted about a position as Executive Director for a nonprofit organization serving people with mental health concerns. The organization, like his, provides housing support along with workforce training and coaching. This would be Jorge's first job at the top of an organization. But the Executive Director role is for an organization with a $10 million budget and 130 staff. In Jorge's current Vice President position he oversees $14 million and more than 200 staff.

You notice the posting for the Executive Director position and want to apply. Jorge will be a candidate—and others like him. If you were the board, who would you hire?

Bessie Collins Johnson

Bessie loved music from her earliest memories. She excelled at piano lessons and voice performances, winning a scholarship to a prominent conservatory where she earned a bachelor's degree in musical performance. With optimism and admittedly some naivete, Bessie set about to change the world by exposing people to the beauty of music.

A few years later, Bessie had experience as a professional musician and a part-time, pro bono music teacher for a youth afterschool program. Bessie loved this work but concluded that while music would remain a major force in her life, it wouldn't be her vocation. She had become active in local politics, including election to the local school board, and she knew she could make a bigger impact in society in other ways.

Many of Bessie's partners in civic activities had law degrees, which nudged Bessie to return to law school to earn a JD. To finance her education, she taught music and worked part-time as an office manager at a local coalition with a mission of ending homelessness.

With her new law degree and variety of work experiences, Bessie began the second chapter of her career with a job in state government. Her position as Program Manager for the state arts board had Bessie evaluating arts programs throughout the state and providing grant funding to the best of them through complex grant arrangements.

Bessie's law degree—with its emphasis on contracts—was coming in handy. Bessie earned a reputation as an adept program leader with uncanny skill for finding emerging arts programs exposing and educating new populations. And she knew how to manage her program budgets.

After eight years, Bessie was asked to oversee her workgroup and was happy to be named Director. By then, she had also joined the boards of two local organizations, a family foundation supporting youth arts education and a local children's museum with a remarkable hands-on learning component.

Some of Bessie's law school friends were earning fat salaries compared to her state government salary. But her work was satisfying and her impact clear.

Bessie wasn't looking for a change, but after a few years as Director, she was contacted by a recruiter to consider a new role as Vice President of Programs at a large regional foundation with a funding emphasis in youth cultural experiences and educational programs. Bessie's state grantmaking work and her knowledge of the regional arts scene were real assets. Her leadership and thoughtful communication style tipped the scales and Bessie was hired.

Bessie has enjoyed five years as Vice President. She's active in the statewide philanthropic member organization, serving on the governance and public policy teams. By this time, she had gained experience in strategic planning, leading the strategy process at her own organization and as a pro bono facilitator for several small arts nonprofits.

While happy in her role, Bessie is starting to think that she's ready to lead an organization. Her background in state and philanthropic funding gives her unique insights into the nonprofit landscape, as does her work on civic boards and committees. Bessie recently learned of an opening for President at a $5 million nonprofit focused on providing educational stipends to underserved youth. These scholarships fund extracurricular programs, primarily in the arts but also in athletics. Bessie is already familiar with the organization and thinks highly of its staff and mission.

You've also seen the posting for this job. You're interested. You submit your resume and think you have a good shot. But Bessie is also a candidate.

Minta Moore

Minta is the Director of Development for the local YWCA, overseeing fundraising of $8.5 million for a $20 million organization. She leads her staff in securing money through government grants, individual and corporate donations, philanthropic foundations, an annual campaign, and three major fundraising events each year. The remainder of the organization's income is earned revenue from its fitness facility and daycare services.

Minta got started in fundraising after earning a degree in art history. With jobs in her field hard to find, Minta became an administrative assistant at a prominent modern art museum. While the job wasn't all she hoped for, Minta loved the museum and its mission. She offered to help other support departments when they were short staffed, and eventually, she was asked to assist with a gala for the museum that, with her help, was the museum's most successful ever.

When Minta was offered a role as Development Coordinator, she accepted, and for the next two years, Minta was closely involved in fundraising events as well as the annual campaign. She attended several seminars and earned a fundraising certification.

A friend connected her to a role as Advancement Manager at a statewide adoption agency. Minta, an adoptee, was passionate about the mission and thrilled about the role. She received a tiny increase on an already small salary, but the work was too meaningful to pass up. In just three years,

Minta doubled the agency's fundraising revenue, leading to an invitation to join the local board of the Association of Fundraising Professionals. Minta was a successful Advancement Manager, and for a year, acted as Interim Executive Director when the organization's leader was on medical leave.

Four years ago, Minta was recruited to the YWCA. It was hard to leave the adoption agency, but Minta felt that she had accomplished her goals and created a top-notch team to carry on the work. Since arriving at the YWCA, Minta has built the fundraising department from the ground up. She hired new staff, reorganized the department, and set a new strategic framework for the development function that aligned with the organization's overall strategic plan.

As a member of senior management in her last two organizations, Minta has partnered with programs and operations, and frequently represented the organization to varied external stakeholder groups. Minta was asked to join the boards of the national YWCA Advancement Associates as well as a local women's shelter. She volunteers as a pro bono fundraising consultant to smaller nonprofits.

You have recently heard about a Vice President of Advancement role, heading up fundraising at a well-known nonprofit in the area. You're a senior sales executive and you're interested in getting into nonprofit. You've never actually done fundraising. But you sense that selling closely resembles fundraising, and you feel many of your skills would transfer.

At the urging of a friend, Minta is strongly considering applying for this Vice President position as well. Minta is the type of candidate you would be competing against if you were to apply. How do you stack up?

Your Best Path Forward

These examples aren't meant to discourage you. Rather, they illustrate how qualified and prepared you usually must be if you're intent about a transition to the nonprofit sector.

So, let's help you prepare to compete with people like Jorge, Bessie, and Minta.

How will you make the jump? What's the best way to learn about potential jobs in the nonprofit sector? How best to investigate and assess your options? And move through the process?

What should you do next?

CHAPTER FIVE

Getting Hired in a Nonprofit Role

You've likely participated in many hiring processes throughout your career from both sides of the table, doing the hiring and hoping to land a role. So you realize that the hiring process, done well, consists of several thoughtful steps. None are pointless hoops. A meaningful process safeguards everyone involved and maximizes the chances of a successful match.

Securing a job in a nonprofit will likely be as complex as getting hired at any other kind of organization. Expect a rigorous search that succeeds or fails based on how you present yourself via a resume and possibly other written narrative... through a telephone screening... and multiple face-to-face interviews.

Let's look at the steps to getting hired in a nonprofit job.

First, in this chapter, we'll consider how to **prepare your resume** so it best communicates your background and interests.

In chapter six, we'll look at the ways to **find and connect to opportunities**—through job postings, recruiters, and your own network.

Lastly, in chapter seven, we'll discuss how you can **prepare and present yourself in face-to-face interviews** for nonprofit roles.

Moving from Here to There

It would be nice if there were a slick repeatable trick I could share for getting hired by a nonprofit organization. There's not!

No secret code.
No special handshake.
And no way around the usual rule:

**Organizations want to hire the most qualified
person with the best organizational fit.**

As you begin your process, it's best not to assume your functional, technical, or subject matter expertise will transfer exactly to the nonprofit sector.

Some functional expertise is more wholly relevant across sectors. Human resources expertise, for example, might be transferrable. So might financial expertise.

Let's consider an example. Say a packaging company goes bankrupt; it is an enterprise with $35 million in annual revenue generated by more than 200 full-time employees and additional seasonal staff. While this is a rather small company in manufacturing and distribution, it would be a sizable social service organization. Nonprofits in education or health care might be significantly larger.

Post-closure, all the various functional Vice Presidents find themselves out of work. Let's posit that all of them are interested in transitioning into the nonprofit sector. All regard themselves as highly desirable executives with backgrounds that will easily transfer to the nonprofit sector.

- The **human resources leader** might find skills such as recruiting, evaluating staff, managing payroll, compensation, and benefits administration transfer well to some nonprofit organizations.

- The **financial leader** might find CFO-type duties share commonalities between sectors. Related background, like early experience auditing nonprofit organizations or serving on nonprofit boards, would be even better.

- The **operations executive**, with content expertise in packaging systems and quality control, might have a more challenging time. Generic traits such as management skills and organizational abilities might be readily transferable. However, a role overseeing operations of an animal shelter or a chamber of commerce would be quite different.

In truth, most parts of most jobs will be different in a nonprofit. The systems differ. So do the processes. The lingo and acronyms are different. How the organization defines "clients" and even how the organization defines or measures "success" varies. For all the general skills and abilities you bring, you're still entering a world that can be radically dissimilar.

Your resume is your opportunity to factually demonstrate your relevance to this new world.

Given that the rules of hiring apply in nonprofits as much as anywhere else, how can you best present yourself to nonprofit organizations?

Preparing Your Resume

Let's start with your resume. You'll need it whether you apply for a position online or connect with a recruiter or a hiring executive.

Let's assume you have a current or relatively recent resume you've used in your business positions. If not, now is the time to create one. Almost always, a chronological, no-nonsense resume laid out in sections (Professional Experience, Education, Civic Activities, etc.) is best.

Should you just use your same corporate resume to apply for nonprofit positions?

For the most part, yes. But any old resume won't do.

Make sure your resume is up-to-the-moment. If you've left your organization, denote the month and year you left. In other words, don't show your former company and position as "present." If you have new activities or credentials, add them as well.

Specifically, ensure you have captured all your nonprofit-related experience, whether gained in a paid role or as a volunteer.

For example, if you've had nonprofit activities or interactions as part of a business job, include them along with other bullets of responsibilities in that role.

Here is a sample layout of a job with nonprofit experience included:

Tech Logic, Inc.   2016 – 2021

Vice President of Business Development

- Reporting to the President, led national team of twenty business development professionals in large account management. Revenue targets of $50 to $75 million.

- Earned quota each year and attended President's Club four years straight.

- Hired and coached staff. Named "Top Manager" of the company in 2017.

- Grew client base in ten new states.

- Achieved all customer service goals in new and existing states.

- **Led the organization's United Way campaign (2018 and 2019). Achieved record employee participation and contribution levels.**

- **Created, along with the Vice President of Engineering, a partner program with two local high schools that included quarterly tours and lunch bag sessions for girls interested in STEM careers.**

If you've had meaningful volunteer experiences, list them as well. These will be particularly relevant, so don't hesitate to show these activities going back 10, 15, even 20 years.

Construct a separate resume section devoted to civic or nonprofit experiences. Here is a sample layout:

Volunteer Community Activities

Big Brothers Big Sisters, Board Member   2018 – Present

Volunteer Big Brother   2010 – 2018

Jazztown Jazz Band, Musician	2015 – Present
Musikids, Program Committee Member	2015 – 2019
Music Matters! Teaching Artist/Musician	2009 – 2013

Should you list donations on your resume?

You may be a generous donor to a particular nonprofit or a person who readily contributes to almost anyone who asks. However, that doesn't belong on a resume. I'm also not keen on really small examples of involvement at a nonprofit appearing on a resume. For example:

- Attended Fundraiser Potluck
  at Our Savior's Church   November 2021

OR

- Participated in a Neighborhood Clean Up Day   October 2020

These activities can be meaningful, and I believe every act of generosity has merit. But resumes are meant to show your most important activities. Think about the highlights you list for your assorted business roles. You wouldn't list a single two-hour activity, for example. Same here. Short-duration activities with limited individual impact should be treasured in your memories but left off your resume. They beg the question, **"THIS is the most important nonprofit activity they can think of?"**

If your volunteerism consists of many of these types of smaller activities, you could combine them all into one line item such as:

Frequent volunteer at local food shelf, neighborhood garden, and cat rescue organization.

Preparing Your Cover Letter

It seems HR professionals and hiring managers either love cover letters or find them irrelevant. You never know if your most painstakingly created message will be read or ignored. At times, a cover letter won't even be required in a hiring process.

Nevertheless, always be ready. Don't dismiss the power of a well-crafted letter to showcase your best. And you'll likely find a use for the same content in a "cover email."

Include a cover letter with your resume if you apply for a role in any formal way. This includes sending materials to a recruiter or executive search firm, a direct application to a human resources department, to some other designee, or to a hiring executive.

A cover letter isn't a repeat of your resume but a reason to read that document, pointing to your resume like a big blinking neon finger.

I'm a fan of relatively straightforward cover letters. The letter shouldn't be more than a page, with ample white space to be inviting.

Lengthy cover letters with stories and detailed narrative are often too much for an introductory piece. I've *never* heard an employer say, "Karen was really the best candidate, but we didn't select her because her cover letter was shorter than the others." Or as a career transition coach told a client who presented him with a three-page cover letter with half-inch margins and 8-point type, "Your mother wouldn't read that."

Here's a model that works well in most situations:

Salutation (Dear Ms., Mr., or Dr.),

Section 1—Your Objective. This is a short paragraph explaining the reason for your correspondence. Not more than a sentence or two. **For example:**

I am pleased to present my credentials in application for the role of President at Family Success.

Section 2—Who You Are. This section includes a paragraph or two summarizing your background. Your resume is likely also included in the correspondence with the cover letter, so don't recap every detail of your resume. However, do include a few sentences reviewing your experience, especially points in your history that have one-to-one correspondence with key needs in the job description of the position you seek. **For example:**

My background includes over twenty years of executive leadership including...

I have general management experience overseeing programs, marketing, HR, IT, and administration at the following organizations...

I've worked for more than two decades in the financial services and financial literacy training field and have led groups of ten to twenty staff members.

Certainly, if you have meaningful experience in the nonprofit sector, you should mention that as well. **For example:**

I have served on the boards of three different advocacy groups, including...

For the past 17 years, I have been an active volunteer team leader at the nonprofit organization Food for All. I have also served on their Program Committee.

While in my corporate roles, I have connected to nonprofit work as the leader of the JMN Foundation, our company's philanthropic organization.

Section 3—Your Connection to the Mission. For many people with business backgrounds and less nonprofit experience, this section is where they hope to make the case about their candidacy. Go ahead. Do it honestly and authentically. Don't oversell. Don't disclose personal details you wouldn't share with people who are, in fact, complete strangers.

Don't think that more persuasion here will win the day. Simply share your genuine connection with the organization's work and mission. Maybe you've been a long-time supporter, volunteer, or donor. Perhaps you or a family member has been impacted by the group's programs and services. Or maybe you're drawn to the mission more generally because you have a long-held commitment to what the organization stands for, whether legal services for recent immigrants, economic opportunities for young entrepreneurs, or safer streets in the urban core. **For example:**

My family and I share a strong connection to the mission of the Leukemia and Lymphoma Society. Our daughter...

Ever since serving in the Peace Corps in the 1980s, I've had a passion for the mission of international relations. In recent years, I have served as statewide program coordinator for two organizations working to build relations between faith communities in our region and abroad.

Fishing, hiking, and wilderness activities have been an important part of my life since I can remember. I share your passion for making these opportunities available to people of all physical abilities.

Section 4—Closing. This is a final statement. You may want to express gratitude for the consideration of your credentials and offer to provide more information if desired.

Don't suggest or dictate the next steps of the process, such as "I would like to set up a meeting with you in the next week or two" or "Please contact me by phone for further discussion." Recently, a corporate applicant for one of our nonprofit CEO opportunities suggested we take down all position postings as she was ready to "help us fill it!"

End with a positive statement of gratitude and your interest in further consideration. **For example:**

Thank you for your kind consideration of my background. I look forward to hearing from you.

I am grateful for the opportunity to share my credentials regarding this role. Please let me know if you have any questions or if I can provide further information.

Highlighting Transferable Skills

A common resume question I get is about highlighting "transferable skills."

We touched on this a moment ago. But how do you best include these skills in your resume?

It's probably true that a good deal of your work experience is transferable. You've learned to navigate relationships and organizations, assess information, and make decisions.

No one would argue that your work experience to this point doesn't have some value in a nonprofit setting or in any work setting for that matter.

Clearly identifying, understanding, and presenting your transferable skills is key evidence of your relevance to a nonprofit role.

So is grasping your limitations and showing authentic readiness to learn from nonprofit experts.

Your transferable skills will probably be apparent to people already working at a nonprofit organization.

- Do you lead training seminars? You likely could deliver planned presentations to community groups at a nonprofit.

- Do you manage a complex customer database? You probably could learn to manage a similar donor database at a community foundation.

- Do you lead the finance function, overseeing multiple department budgets? You'll probably discover that's entirely relevant at a comparably sized nonprofit.

These examples are immediately obvious hard skills. You use them now. You would use them in a similar way in a new role. You wouldn't have to worry about convincing others that these are transferable.

Be aware of what aspects of your current experience fall into the category of immediately obvious hard skills for a nonprofit role. What do I mean by that? Only label them as immediately obvious transferable hard skills if you know for a fact they are. You'll need a decent sense of the nonprofit role you're considering and the specific work responsibilities. Do your homework. Call your network. Get some feedback.

People also ask me about high-level skills like "organizational leadership." Aren't those transferable?

Sure. If you manage a staff of ten people now, attributes might transfer if a potential nonprofit role has a staff of nine.

On the surface, this seems to be highly transferable. But let's look at an example:

- What if your current staff are civil engineers and the new staff would be direct service staff for individuals with cognitive disabilities?

- What if your current staff works in a high-rise headquarters and the new staff are disbursed in three group homes?

- What if your current staff are highly paid with an average tenure of six-plus years vs. the new staff who are low-paid and move on every six months?

How transferable is the skill of staff management in the above scenario?

Squishy, right?

Certainly, knowing how to manage staff has value. Yet the business management background I described is wildly different from the nonprofit management setting. Could you really jump into managing in this new situation? Would you want to?

Here's another one. Let's say that you believe you've developed a tremendous sense of teamwork. That's transferable, right?

Well, yes. What organization doesn't want great teamwork?

But what if your current team is international? What if you've worked out a creative way to connect for checkpoint meetings in different time zones so all members are included? What if you have come up with an online communication tool that all members can contribute to daily? What if you have expensive, highly technical project tracking software that each team uses to measure progress?

Then—what if the new team is a group of college-age volunteers assisting at a local Boys and Girls Club? What if their work is fluid and undefined? Will the teamwork abilities you've developed play out in the same way? Are your teamwork skills better or more "transferable" than similar skills brought by other candidates?

What I think about transferable skills is this:

All your prior work experience and learning has value.
You're a product of your many years in specific roles with specific people.
You have many skills and abilities.
Many of your skills are immediately and obviously related.
No effort will be required to explain how they apply.
That's great!

Other skills aren't so clearly relevant.
Maybe they will be transferable.
Maybe partially transferable.
Maybe not!

Will you have more or better transferable skills than other candidates?
Impossible to know.

Candidates often overemphasize the transferability of their abilities. Don't! Realize the skills you see as transferable are often those possessed in equal measure by other candidates. Come into the process with a holistic sense of self and a confident yet humble assessment of how you might stand in comparison to others.

How about your backstory or passion for the mission? Isn't that compelling?

Yes! Let's spend a minute on how you can most effectively incorporate your personal passion and connection to a nonprofit's mission.

We've already talked about how a vague assertion that you are "mission driven" will do you more harm than good. It's bland. It's predictable. Worse, it communicates nothing.

It's crucial that any leader at a nonprofit have a strong affinity for the mission. It almost goes without saying. But in your case, it's not as easy to *state* and *demonstrate*. Why? Because the narrative for someone moving from the corporate sector to the nonprofit world must explain the *Why?*

Why am I taking a cut in pay to take on a job where I won't be an expert? *Why indeed!*

Presumably, a major motivation for considering a lower paying, equally stressful, and potentially more taxing role is your draw to the mission. You see needs out in the world. You care deeply about the work. You feel compelled to be a part of the solution. If this isn't indeed the case for you in a specific situation, perhaps you should stop the process and examine your own *Why?*

You'll be asked about this. Guaranteed. And rightly so.

Nonprofits know this:

- Passion for mission draws staff together to work in difficult situations for low pay.

- Passion for mission pulls staff in on weekends or whenever the need arises.

- Passion for mission fuels the hard work and perseverance required to engage human suffering.

- Passion for mission is a key driver in the nonprofit sector.

- Passion for mission will be explored as part of a hiring process, because without passion, you'll fail to fit and you'll fail at the job.

So how can you best share your passion for the mission of an organization?

- First, **know precisely what that mission is.** I often converse with individuals who incorrectly state the mission of an organization. They mistake advocacy for direct service. They make assumptions about the focus or direction of an organization. Their perception of an organization is dated and no longer accurate.

There's an easy fix. Do your homework. A thorough review of the nonprofit's website is a good starting point. Look through their financial records and strategic plan. See what the organization puts in writing and how it markets itself.

- Second, **articulate a true connection to the mission with examples from your lived experience.**

For example, sharing your passion as "I love kids" is weak if you're applying to join the camps division of your state YMCA. Much stronger is "I've been associated with Y camps my whole life as a camper and camp counselor and now camp parent. Y camp has had a profound impact on me and my family." A similar statement would help in related organizations as well.

On almost every search, I'm contacted by people "interested" in a role who can't articulate a specific connection to the mission of the organization. They say things like:

- "I believe in equality and opportunity for everyone."

- "I'm passionate about our region and seek to make it better."

- "I love music and always have."

- "I would like to 'give back' and 'make a difference.'"

These comments aren't bad. They might be uttered with all seriousness. But other candidates will express much more compelling commitments to the mission. Compare those weak comments to the following:

- "I was raised by two parents who were executives at the NAACP. I stuffed envelopes, handed out flyers at rallies, and was a general gofer throughout my childhood. As an adult, I've devoted most of my volunteerism to groups focused on equity and inclusion."

- "I'm a lifelong resident of Chicago and passionate about the city. I was a 'parks kid' and took advantage of all that our park system had to offer. The last few years, I've given a lot of attention to the lakeshore area and various initiatives to keep the area clean and vibrant."

- "I'm an experienced piano player and vocalist. As a hobby, I've assisted my brother in restoring heritage pianos. Music education is near to my heart and something I still do as a guest speaker and performer for an arts high school here in the city."

- "My grandmother lived with us growing up and I've always had a passion for older adults. I was a candy striper and volunteer with older adults through high school and college. My mother lives with us now. I am passionate about multi-generational living."

We've talked about making sure your resume includes your nonprofit and civic involvement. Ideally, your activities and volunteerism have mirrored your areas of interest and passion. You can point to several examples of how you have lived out or furthered your connection to the mission.

What if you don't have any real connection to the mission of the organization you seek to join?

That could happen. A couple suggestions.

First, think about what connections you *do* have. For example, let's say you're applying for a job at Habitat for Humanity. You've never been involved in the housing sector, and you're not even terribly handy.

Dig deeper. What appeals to you about this organization? What ignited your interest?

- Perhaps you're passionate about your city. You've been active in several initiatives to improve the region's livability. Affordable housing is part of that equation.

- Maybe you've focused on volunteerism related to women and children. Families are stronger when they have stable housing. That could be a legitimate connection.

- Perhaps you've experienced housing insecurity. How did you benefit when housing became stable? If that isn't a connection, I don't know what is.

If your connection to the mission sounds generic, you either haven't struggled hard enough to be clear or you've stretched a point too far.

You'll agree that a comment like "I'm interested in this position because I want to give back" is tepid. "I really care about people" is also too vague.

If you truly don't have any connection with the mission of the nonprofit via volunteerism or personal experience, don't force it. Definitely don't make something up!

If you can't find a meaningful connection to the work of the organization, keep up your homework. Read the website. Read new articles. Ask around. Then listen to your heart. What resonates? What connects?

Keep at it until you have a real and meaningful statement of how you connect with the work. It might not be lengthy. It might not be overly personal—or it could be incredibly personal, like, "I'm a breast cancer survivor committed to helping others maintain positivity and normalcy as they go through medical treatment."

Whatever your passion for the organizational mission, include it. Essential!

What if you have scant nonprofit exposure—much less experience?

If you've worked through preparing your resume and realized you have little to no connection to the nonprofit world, I must be honest that you're at an obvious disadvantage compared to other candidates.

If you've picked up this book, I'm assuming two things. First, you have skills you've practiced in a business setting. Those are real skills. Second, you have more than a passing interest in find your place in the nonprofit world, or at least considering it as a possibility. That's real heart.

But as a leader, you do have to consider this: Think about how you would react if you were hiring an Engineering Manager and an applicant had no formal background or training in engineering. Would you consider this candidate? Could you? What about if they wrote an impassioned cover letter about their passion for the engineering field? Would that sway you?

Nowhere will your relative lack of credentials be more obvious than when resumes are laid side-by-side in an application process. You might have a killer resume for your usual sector, but it likely won't stand up against those of people who've spent years building credentials in the nonprofit sector. I say this not to be negative but to be realistic. When it comes to sending resumes in for consideration against other candidates, your background and experience won't likely hold its usual sway.

That said, it doesn't hurt to try. You will learn by doing. How should you describe your connection to this job, this work, this mission? What roles might be the closest fit? Am I overestimating my level of "fit" compared to other applicants?

Maybe it's just one job in the nonprofit world that caught your attention. What other jobs are out there for which you might be best suited?

Whatever the case, any real job search in the nonprofit sector means searching the field and discovering the breadth of what's possible. In the next chapter, we'll look at how to unearth those roles.

CHAPTER SIX

Searching for Nonprofit Roles

Starting your job search online is a reflex. Want a new job? Open a browser and commence hunting!

That said, I want to convince you to right-size your expectations about the value of "answering ads" as a strategy for entering the nonprofit sector.

What? Isn't going online modern life's solution to pretty much everything? That's how most of us discover job opportunities, right?

Occasionally. People do connect with organizations and land jobs through postings. Statistically, however, that approach doesn't add up to many landings. Evidence shows that job postings alone have relatively little value for people hoping to find a new job in a nonprofit.

Looking for your next role through postings could be a starting point, perhaps. Or it might be a way to nose around the market.

My point?

Please don't use online ads as your one-and-done attempt to find a nonprofit role.

It's tough to resist the lure of potential jobs posted online. So if you browse, at least dig in the right places. Ask around to uncover sites that contain your region's most robust lists of nonprofit jobs. Look too at national job sites in specific categories, such as "immigration legal services" or "youth camp directors" or whatever terms best describe your target role.

In any field, higher-level jobs are difficult to land through an ad, and your desire to jump to a nonprofit role creates an additional challenge.

You're attempting a big change. And the built-in process of replying to job postings makes it especially difficult to translate your experience in business organizations to nonprofit work.

Imagine this scenario.

You see a job posting for an Executive Director of a small nonprofit called Music4Success. For 30 years, this organization has brought music education to schools through innovative volunteer-led seminars.

The role looks interesting. While you've never run a nonprofit, you feel your business skills in sales and marketing are highly transferable. You've managed groups of sales professionals much larger than this organization's staff. You were active in the Parent-Teacher organization for your child's school. As an off-and-on piano player for most of your life, you relish music of all types.

Based on your self-assessment of fit, you submit your application for the Executive Director role.

It's not hard for me to picture what's probably on the receiving end of that application: a nervous board of directors. Even though a staff person or board member might be temporarily holding the organization together, the board is focused on hiring the next permanent Executive Director. ASAP. They engaged a consultant to help write the job description, then posted the opportunity on a variety of nonprofit and general employment sites.

You can assume the posting has caught the eye of many job seekers, and sure enough, several dozen people apply. Those are normal numbers. At a minimum.

We've all heard about the difficulty of finding talent and that many posted positions go unfilled. That's true, although Executive Director roles in nonprofit organizations aren't usually those types of jobs.

Ads draw a large applicant pool. And that's a significant challenge if your job search relies on postings alone to break through to your next role.

The quantity of job seekers, however, is just the first challenge of applying through postings. In the nonprofit world, as in most of the job market, you're also up against the quality of the applicants.

In this case, many applicants have relevant nonprofit experience in other youth-serving organizations. Others are former music teachers with leadership background from avocational and civic activities. These are qualified candidates from the nonprofit sector who seek a change or are ready to step up to the Executive Director role.

Several are businesspeople like you.

Remember my earlier comments about the tsunami of business leaders seeking to move into the nonprofit sector? Many applicants score bonus points for serving on boards of arts or education-based nonprofits. Some have led significant fundraising activities for major nonprofit expansions.

All those people are applying. If you answer an ad, that's your competition!

Back to our scenario. The Human Resources Representative at Music4Success is tasked with reviewing resumes, and your well-tuned document sits in a pile with those of other applicants.

The Human Resources Representative at Music4Success thoughtfully reviews the resumes of dozens of applicants, searching for the dozen or so best-qualified candidates to share with the board of director's Human Resources committee, who will further study the candidates and contact those they wish to interview.

This brings up the second challenge of job postings. As your resume is being reviewed, you aren't on hand to explain how your background translates to the nonprofit sector and to this specific job. The connection might be readily apparent to you, but it isn't likely so obvious to others. In your cover letter, you can and should attempt to capture the correlations between your past work and this job. But that's frequently hard to do. Things get lost in translation.

That's the rub. A posting represents an open role, an actual opportunity that needs to be filled. The organization has every intention of filling it. But if you access a hiring process only by tossing in your resume, then YOU aren't there to explain to the Human Resources Representative how your background transfers to the Executive Director spot at Music4Success. You have no way to personally describe your ability to learn quickly—or to detail any of the other qualities you want to emphasize.

I don't love the idea that someone is reviewing my background and resume without me there to explain it. I don't have confidence when I'm stuck in a vacuum.

I don't like the odds of applying for jobs through job postings.

There are a couple other main pathways to a nonprofit role.

Working With Recruiters

The world at large often calls recruiters "headhunters." I don't love the term, but as a member of the recruiting profession, I hear it plenty.

"What do you do?" people ask me.

"I work in executive search." Blank stare.

"I do recruiting," I clarify.

"Oh, you're a headhunter!" comes the response.

"Yes, I suppose I am," I reluctantly agree.

I understand where the term "headhunter" comes from. Recruiters hunt for people. We're hired, often at considerable cost, to recruit candidates with skills highly suited to a particular job. Client organizations carefully spell out the background, experience, credentials, and characteristics required to succeed in a role. Before we begin to look for candidates, we try to meet with an abundance of people across a hiring organization to get a firsthand feel for the organization's culture.

Once we begin recruiting for a position, we call dozens or even hundreds of people to find an appropriate slate of candidates.

As a recruiter, my personal record for calling potential candidates is 550. I feel a need to spell that out. FIVE HUNDRED AND FIFTY CALLS. For ONE role!

That sounds unhinged. But it took those hundreds of calls in search of a Vice President of Human Resources role at an international manufacturing firm to assemble a group of qualified candidates to present to my client. Granted, the role required highly unique skills and experiences.

But for any given search, recruiters usually contact and consider a large if not overwhelming number of candidates, all to find individuals closely aligned with client specifications.

I can guess what you're thinking. "That's interesting, Marcia, but what does it mean for me?"

Well, a few things. Consider these points.

- First, **recruiters work for the organization that has hired them.** The organization hires and pays the search firm. The organization is the client.

In other words, **there isn't a client relationship between recruiters and candidates.**

At times, it might seem as if you have a recruiter working for you or looking for a job for you. You might connect occasionally with a recruiter or get to know that person well. It's great if you have positive relationships with recruiters. The recruiter may even have said you have exceptional skills. But don't ever be confused. The recruiter works for the hiring organization.

- Second, **consider why an organization is compelled to hire a recruiter.** Paying for recruitment assistance typically only happens when an organization has difficulty filling the position on its own.

Why? A role might be unique. Candidates with a specific background might be scarce. An incumbent's unexpected resignation or illness might create urgency. Or time sensitivity around an impending audit or launch of a capital campaign, for example, requires a fully qualified candidate able to hit the ground running.

In any case, the organization expects a recruiter to seek on their behalf candidates with the requisite skills, background, and characteristics needed to do the job. Recruiters are given detailed specifications about what's needed for success, and **the deal is we agree to recruit those types of candidates.**

The upshot for you? Recruiters almost never have the latitude to recruit and present people whose experience isn't closely related to requirements of the open position. Their contract, in fact, says they will only bring candidates forward qualified to do the job. And most recruiters warranty their work, paying back their fee if a candidate washes out within a specified period. You might feel your experience is transferable, but the recruiter needs certainty just as much as the organization does.

- Lastly, **keep in mind that only a very small percentage of all positions are filled through search firms.** Typically, only full-time, higher-level roles are available through recruiters. You won't find part-time or project positions through a search firm, and you won't find interim or consulting gigs. Think about connecting with search firms only relating to senior level, full-time roles.

As with applying to postings, the odds of accessing a job through a search firm alone are a long shot. But it does help to understand the answers to a few key questions.

What Exactly Will Search Firms Do for Me?

Two situations determine the response you can expect.

The first case is when you proactively connect with the search firm to share your background and inquire if they have an active search that might fit for your interests.

If you aren't an immediate fit for any of the search firm's active searches, many firms will do little or nothing *for* you. They will, however, often do the following:

- Receive your resume if you send it to them, typically by email.

- Acknowledge receipt of your resume.

- Enter the resume into their active database.

- Point you to website information about current searches or other helpful information.

That's it. You shouldn't expect the firm to do things like review and edit your resume, meet to provide career advice, or direct you to other sources of possible jobs. Search firms aren't career consultants or resume writers. They don't typically make time to help you connect with their competitors in the search industry. Those activities are all up to you. There are excellent career transition consultants out there, and they will be happy to assist you.

Don't ask search firms to provide these services. We recently had a person contact our firm with a request to be added to our database. He also asked for his resume to be reviewed, edited, and redesigned.

We were quick to say...NO! Nicely, of course.

The second situation is when you contact a search firm—or the firm reaches out to you—and you become a potential or active candidate for a current project. In that case, the search firm might do most or all of the following things for you:

- Send you a job description or position profile for the search under consideration.

- Interview you to get to know you better and discuss your credentials and background.

- Disclose client requirements for the role along with an honest assessment of your fit.

- Share the timeline for the search and other logistical considerations.

- Advise you if your resume needs revision and suggest improvements.

- Prepare you for interviews or interactions with the client organization.

- Give you feedback throughout the process.

- Guide you through any tricky situations that might arise.

These activities are common ways a recruiter will work with you as a potential candidate (investigating a search opportunity) or a candidate (pursuing a search opportunity).

Remember, however, if you connect with the search firm simply to make yourself known to them as a future potential candidate, the interaction with them will be short and transactional. That's not an insult to your credentials or a snap judgment of your value in the market. It's simply how firms who are heads-down on current searches gather basic information for their database. Later, if you're a potential candidate or active candidate on a search, you'll work closely with the recruiter and get to know them well.

How Should I Make Myself Known to Search Firms?

The best way to initially connect with search firms is via email. Recruiters wish they had time to meet in person with every potential candidate, but they field a lot of requests and that isn't usually possible.

Email the search firm and attach your resume, ideally in both Word and PDF formats. You might have the name of a specific person to contact. If you don't, sending an email and resume to a general company email (like info@ballingerleafblad.com) is just fine too.

In your message, note that you're seeking a new opportunity in the nonprofit sector. Share your background and experience in summary form.

Close on a positive note, offering to provide more information or answer any questions.

You might hear back from the search firms with a return email noting receipt of your resume. You might get a call from a recruiter with immediate questions about your background. You might not hear anything for a while. Don't feel bad. Search firms are usually very small, with only a handful of staff. Administrative activities like following up with potential candidates can take a while.

Which Search Firms Should I Contact?

Do you wonder which search firms are the best to contact? I contend that there aren't necessarily some firms that are better than others. When you're looking for a job, every search firm is a good search firm!

If you live in a larger urban area, some search firms—like mine—might specialize in recruiting for nonprofit organizations. Contact those firms for sure. But many search firms don't name a specialty—give them a try as well. Generalist search firms hunt for candidates for roles in multiple sectors, including nonprofits.

Websites like customdatabanks.com offer lists of executive search firms by location or sector.

Should I Contact the Search Firm to Let Them Know I'm Still Looking?

That's a variation on a common question: "How often should I contact search firms to check my information is still in their database?" I have a ready answer. I'm not trying to be snarky but to nail the point. My reply: "How often do you call your credit card company to make sure you're still in their database?"

No credit card company will cut you from their database. Nor will any search firm!

Recruiters take their database seriously and manage it carefully. They typically keep potential candidate information for years. I've never known a search firm to delete people.

While it isn't necessary for you to check your record, do keep firms up-to-date about key details like changes in contact information, employment status, or job title. If you earn an additional degree or professional credential, or gain significant new civic experience, for example, as a board director or elected official, add that to your resume and send us a new version.

Search firms are glad to amend your file when significant changes occur.

Other than that, rest assured your information is accurate and active.

What About "Don't Call Us, We'll Call You"?

A candidate told me that when she contacted another area recruiter, he told her point blank, "Don't call us, we'll call you!" She wondered if that could possibly be true. Do recruiters really feel that way?

I'm known as a straight shooter, and here is my straight answer: That statement is partly true. At least as it relates to recruiting for senior executives.

Remember that recruiters are paid to find hard-to-find people and engage them in dialogue. These leaders are usually successful and happy in their current role, in part because they possess unique specialized skills related to the job at hand. Clients pay search firms for this service. Scouring every possible source to find leaders with specialized backgrounds and skills is how that happens.

Executive recruiting starts and ends with research. What organizations do potential candidates work for? What are their titles? What trade/member/professional groups do they belong to? What do they read? What conferences do they attend? What credentials or certifications have they earned? And so on.

We use lists, databases, the internet, library resources, and other diverse techniques. Done right, research is thoughtful and complex.

Do we look at LinkedIn? Yes. To increase the odds you can be found by executive search firms—or organizations searching on their own—make sure your LinkedIn profile is attractive and complete.

Search firms can do great work and find outstanding candidates even if they don't accept unsolicited resumes. If you're doing the right kind of work, they'll find you. I'm certain that's the sentiment behind the words reported to me.

Candidate databases aren't the primary source of finding qualified candidates. That's the unvarnished reality.

That said, as a recruiter I constantly build my database. Why? I never know what might happen. Occasionally, a strong candidate emerges from our database, someone who sent their resume to us unsolicited.

So do contact all the search firms on your list. It only takes a few minutes to craft an email and attach a resume. You might get valuable feedback or ignite a useful conversation. You might learn about opportunities you might consider or participate as a candidate. You never know!

Networking Your Way to Your Nonprofit Job

We've established the difficulty of finding a nonprofit leadership role from online postings or through executive search firms.

All is not lost.

Your best path to a nonprofit leadership role is open to everyone. Your biggest ally in finding a job in the nonprofit sector is your network. People you already know—and the people they know, and those they know, and so on—have wisdom, ideas, referrals, and perhaps job suggestions. This is freely available to you for the asking.

Networking to the rescue!

A decade ago, I wrote the first edition of the book *The 20-Minute Networking Meeting: How Little Meetings Can Lead to Your Next Big Job.* The book came out just as the world was emerging from the most brutal years of the Great Recession, and the content is as relevant now as then.

In my work as a recruiter across diverse fields, I had experienced—*endured*—thousands of networking meetings. Honestly, many meetings left me frustrated. Not just for myself and the time I had spent, but for the person who had sought my help. The connecting sessions were unfocused, inefficient, rarely as powerful as they could be. So in the book I present a power-packed one-to-one networking process that can be accomplished in 20 minutes.

Smart networking is effective. It's good that little meetings can still lead to your next big job.

Organizations that track mechanisms for obtaining professional jobs routinely show 75 to 80 percent of all jobs are obtained through networking. Wow! Think about it.

Of all the ways you can hunt for your next role, you're *very highly likely* to land your next opportunity through networking.

Networking can be intimidating. The idea of calling total strangers and asking for a job opportunity is scary. I'm happy to tell you effective networking doesn't focus on calling people you don't know or with whom you don't have a meaningful connection. And in your networking meetings, the one thing you won't ask for is a job. No feeling like you're begging!

Not ask for a job? Isn't that the point?

I hope you'll read *The 20-Minute Networking Meeting* sooner rather than later. It's a quick read crucial to making a jump to the nonprofit world.

Let's talk about networking and how to do it well. Let me sum up several straightforward tips and techniques.

What Is Networking?

I define networking as a process of building and enhancing relationships with an emphasis on connecting with people who might have thoughts, ideas, or referrals related to your job search.

Networking is about gaining wisdom and information. And isn't that super important to you right now? You want insights into topics like

- Where would I fit in the nonprofit sector?

- What places might be best?

- What organizations connect with my mission?

- What should I watch out for?

- Should I do this?!?

Networking is also about making new contacts and connections. You'll want a broad array of people to weigh in with advice, ideas, and suggestions for your journey. Eventually, your network will grow from people you already know to people you don't know but who have been recommended to you.

Lastly, networking is about making a great impression out in the talent marketplace. You want to know people and you want to be known. When a networking interaction is over, you want the other person to have a positive impression. You want them to remember you. You want them, ideally, to refer you to others.

Who Should I Network With?

Your network is bigger than you think. I promise. Consider who you know that might have wisdom, ideas, perspectives, or referrals. Who could be aware of a job that might interest you? Who is associated with a nonprofit organization, either on staff or on the board? Who do you know that volunteers regularly? Who has been the recipient of services from a nonprofit?

Networking contacts might include:

- Friends

- Family members

- Neighbors

- Work colleagues, former colleagues

- Connections from your faith community

- Other parents from your children's school

- People with shared hobbies, interests, and values (veterans' groups, alma mater, etc.)

The best method of networking is through individual meetings. It's how you'll learn meaningful information and gather meaningful connections related to the nonprofit sector.

What About Networking at Conferences and Events?

Networking at large group events can be a fine supplement to individual meetings. Think about organizations in your area that sponsor events related to the nonprofit sector. You can attend events with interesting speakers and discussion topics that add to your knowledge and simultaneously meet people and make new connections.

The practice of networking at big tent events is often a brief affair consisting of a quick hello followed by an exchange of business cards. That isn't networking. A two-minute conversation doesn't give you meaningful new information. Nor does the other person learn anything about you. But meeting contacts and exchanging cards at an event is a first step.

Immediately after the event—same day or next day—connect on LinkedIn with the people you met. Include a brief note. "I enjoyed meeting you at the event last evening and would like to stay connected on LinkedIn."

Within a few days, follow up your new connections to request a one-on-one meeting. You might have mentioned this when you met at the event. "You have an interesting background, Ingrid. I'd love to get together some time in person to learn more."

How Should I Request a Networking Meeting?

I think email works well for initiating networking meetings. A few tips:

- While you might feel urgency to learn about opportunities in the nonprofit sector, your networking contact likely has a full schedule. Make your request to meet in the next several weeks, not the next few days.

- If you've been referred to a networking contact, make sure you mention that fact:

  "Sam Washington suggested I connect with you. He had high praise for your sales leadership skills and your commitment to giving back to the community on the board of the local American Red Cross."

"Geneva Yuen says hello! She suggested that I connect with you because of your years of service at workforce development organizations."

- Make meeting easy for the other party. You can meet virtually, by Zoom, Microsoft Teams, or another platform (of the other person's choosing, of course). If you and your networking contact want to connect in person, offer to meet at their office. Don't ask to meet near your home or "halfway between our locations." You're requesting the meeting, so you must accommodate the meeting.

- Ask for no more than a half hour for your meeting. A great networking meeting doesn't need to take a long time.

How Should I Prepare for a Networking Meeting?

Prepare for a networking meeting two ways.

First, try to learn about the person you will be meeting. You might be planning a networking conversation with your BFF, but it's more likely that you'll meet with someone you don't know particularly well.

Look at their LinkedIn profile. Note the jobs they have had and where they have worked. What's their educational background, whether formal academic degrees or seminars or certificates? See if they list any avocational activities, such as hobbies, board positions, or other volunteerism. Do they follow any thought leaders?

Do an online search. Is there other information available, like a bio on their organization's website or articles or speaking engagements?

Note where you have similarities. ("Hey, we are both electrical engineers by training!"). Note areas where you might wish to learn more. ("Hmmm... he moved from landscape architecture to facilities management.")

Second, plan a few questions that you would like to ask the individual.

Thinking about their unique background and experiences, what do you sincerely want to learn from this person? Don't plan questions calculated to impress, and don't ask anything you could easily learn elsewhere (such as "What's the current enrollment at your college?").

Bring at least two and no more than four questions to the networking meeting.

What Should I Say in the Networking Meeting?

Start by saying thank you. Remind the person of how you are connected. ("If you'll recall, we were introduced by Buddy Harper. I also noticed that we're both alums of North Carolina State.") Let the person know you're seeking to network and gain some of their insights... and that you've come prepared with a few questions.

Share a little bit about yourself, keeping it short. No more than a minute! This isn't the time to fully review your resume. A super quick overview will do. Something like: "Just for a bit of context, I worked in county government for over 20 years, mostly in the public works arena. My most recent position was as Public Works Director. On the side, I've been active in fraternal organizations such as the Shriners."

Next, ask your planned questions, such as, "You've been on the board of both the state Chamber of Commerce as well as the city Chamber of Commerce. I'm wondering about how those experiences have been for you?"

Watch the clock. It's quite possible you won't get through all your questions or topics. You might feel like you're cutting off a robust discussion. That's okay. You promised a short, targeted meeting, and you will deliver.

How Should I Follow Up After the Meeting?

Follow up after the meeting with a note or message—email is fine—thanking the individual and referring to something special you learned from the meeting.

After that, follow up when you have a meaningful reason to do so. This might include passing along a greeting and compliment from a mutual friend. It might be sharing an article that could be of interest. Never follow up just to "stay in front" of the individual.

Is Networking Different in the Nonprofit Sector vs. the For-Profit Sector?

Not really. Networking is networking, whether you're seeking a new job, a consulting gig, a board position, or anything else. The purpose of networking is to gain wisdom, get insights, and possibly add new contacts. Connecting with people who possess valuable information, insights, and contacts is always a good idea, and the basic nature of networking transcends the specific purpose.

Just a reminder:

The one thing you will NEVER ask in a networking meeting is this: "Do you have a job opening?" or "Do you know of a job?"

Trust me. No one wants to be put on the spot and asked to find you a new job.

Make your networking meetings about seeking wisdom. Keep the emphasis on building a relationship and learning from the other person.

You'll find that by *not asking* for a job (making the other person uncomfortable) you'll get *more* suggestions and ideas leading you to potential jobs.

If your networking is successful, you will meet any number of amazing people. You'll learn from their experiences. You'll get suggestions and tips you can apply. You'll gain wisdom. If you're like most active job networkers, you'll also get connected to great new job opportunities.

At the end of the day, whether you become a candidate through applying online (a long shot), working with a search firm (also a long shot), or networking (a better shot), you'll need to interview to get the job.

Next up, let's talk about interviews.

CHAPTER SEVEN

Nailing the Interview

However you arrived here—responding to online postings, partnering with a recruiter, networking, or a combination of these things—you've secured an interview. Congratulations!

That's no small thing. Perhaps the trick was energetically networking, making meaningful contacts in the nonprofit sector. Or your past volunteerism or board work spotlighted you as a candidate for an open position. Possibly, you've shored up your resume and submitted an impressive cover letter in response to an online posting.

However you arrived here, getting to the interview stage is a big deal.

You know intuitively the stakes just rose, along with your excitement and, possibly, anxiety. I can promise this: With thoughtful preparation, you'll be ready to perform your best.

Putting an Interview in Context

Of all the components in a hiring process, the most impactful—for the hiring organization—is the interview.

No matter how

spiffy your RESUME
pithy your COVER LETTER
gushing your REFERENCES
stellar your ASSESSMENT RESULTS

the INTERVIEW will be more impactful in an organization's decision to hire you.

How, then, should you think about an interview? What mental frame can you put around your upcoming discussion?

Think about an interview like this: It's a conversation.

This all-important discussion is an occasion for two parties—you and the interviewer or interviewing team—to roam across a variety of subjects, including the open position, your interest in the organization and role, your qualifications and fit, and a variety of related topics.

Make no mistake, however. This conversation is led by the other party. As with networking, my rule about running the meeting still holds ("Whoever calls the meeting runs the meeting"). The interviewer called the meeting and will take the lead. Leading will mostly take the form of questions asked by the interviewer(s). But how the meeting starts, topics covered, and everything else should also be directed by the other party.

CAUTION: If you find yourself sliding into the driver's seat and grabbing the steering wheel, you're in trouble. In my 25 years of sitting in on candidate interviews—a couple hundred each year—I have NEVER seen a candidate who attempts to seize control of an interview be invited back.

The following reality is contrary to what many assume, but an interview is NEVER about persuasion. Remember, it's a conversation, one led by the other party at that. It's never an opportunity for a candidate to "take the stage" and "make their case." If a candidate says to me, "Just let me in front of your client, and I'll convince them I'm the one," I know I can't put the candidate in front of my client. At least not without significant coaching.

The interview conversation, while professional, should feel friendly and natural. More than likely there has been considerable thought about broad topics to discuss and specific questions to ask. Go with the flow. Never take over the interview and turn it into a persuasive pitch about your credentials and fit.

I've been known to tell people if they find themselves attempting to persuade in an interview, they should close their portfolio, say thanks, and exit. Because it's over.

So, if your job isn't to persuade, sway, convince, or otherwise campaign, what can you do?

The first thing you can do is prepare.

Preparing for the Interview

Before your meeting, make sure you know as much as you can about the organization, the job, and the people you are meeting.

It's impossible to know everything about an organization in advance of an interview, but you absolutely should understand the basics. Use any online resources, printed organizational material, and input from people involved with the organization to get the best sense of the place and its purpose.

What to look for? Context. The big picture. And any details that fill out your sense of the organization.

Here are some examples of what you should investigate before an interview:

The organization's website

- What is the organization's stated mission?

- Whom does it serve?

- What are the primary programs and services?

- How large is the organization (in terms of budget, staff size, and geographic reach)?

- Who is on the organization's leadership team? What are their backgrounds?

The organization's Form 990 financial report (this should be readily available online for most nonprofits)

- What is the organization's most recent revenue? Is it rising or falling from years past?

- What are the primary sources of revenue?

- How much does the organization pay its senior executives? Is this what you expected?

- Any spending categories that surprise you? Anything else of note?

The organization's LinkedIn/Facebook profile

- How is the organization presenting itself?

- What is the "vibe"?

- Who in your network is connected with this organization?

If you know whom you're meeting, look them up as well. What is their role in the organization (staff or board)? How long have they been associated with the organization? What is their background and experience? Do you have anything in common?

Job Match Matrix

Before the interview, it's crucial to reflect on your own fit for this role. To start, carefully review the job description, position profile, or any other information you have about the potential role.

In my book *Winning the Executive Interview,* I suggest you begin assessing your fit by creating a grid I call the Job Match Matrix. In the process of creating a grid, you can gauge areas of strong fit for the position and the areas of lesser fit where you would need assistance. It's vital you identify both!

The first column lists the primary qualifications sought by the organi-zation. If you have a job description or position profile, study it carefully. Use the list of required experience and qualifications to create the first column of a grid.

For example:

JOB MATCH MATRIX		
Qualification/ Requirement		
Ten years of nonprofit leadership experience		
Ten years of experience in disability services		
Experience with fundraising, particularly a capital campaign		
Experience setting strategy; working with a board of directors		

The second column should capture your qualifications. Note too your specific results in this area. If you're moving from the for-profit to the nonprofit sector, expect that your experience and results won't match exactly. Don't overstate your experience! List your related experience exactly as it is.

This is your opportunity to rigorously examine your fit, knowing your interviewers will do the same. For example:

JOB MATCH MATRIX		
Qualification/ Requirement	**Experience/Results**	
Ten years of nonprofit leadership experience	No direct nonprofit leadership experience. 25 years of experience leading large teams of technology professionals. 5 years of board service— youth leadership program.	

Ten years of experience in disability services	No work experience in this area.	
Experience with fundraising, particularly a capital campaign	Some fundraising as a board member at Coats for Kids and Animal Rescue Dakotas. No capital campaigns.	
Experience setting strategy; working with a board of directors	I'm on the strategy committee for my company and lead the strategic planning process. I attend and present at all board meetings. Many years of nonprofit board experience, including strategic planning.	

Use the third column to jot down additional commentary or narrative related to that category. You might not have **direct experience** in the area (preferred) but you might have related or **tangential experience** (acceptable). You may also have **lived experience** connecting you to this mission. I'm an adoptive parent, for example, and thus connected to the category of adoption services. Or you might have **other related experiences** not captured in traditional work.

Also—and this is important—**give yourself a rating on each of the qualification areas**—of high/medium/low (or H/M/L) in each category.

For all candidates, even those immediately and obviously qualified for a specific job, I require at least one category receive a HIGH rating and at least one category receive a LOW rating. This is very important.

As someone seeking to move into a new sector, don't be frustrated if you have several low or medium ratings. As a matter of fact, I would expect you to have several of each! Being keenly aware of where you fit and where you might need assistance is an asset. Trust me, it will be to your advantage to take a hard yet accurate look at yourself in these categories before you're face-to-face with your interviewers.

Here's what a filled-in third column might look like:

JOB MATCH MATRIX		
Qualification/ Requirement	Experience/Results	
Ten years of nonprofit leadership experience	No direct nonprofit leadership experience. 25 years of experience leading large teams of technology professionals. 5 years of board service— youth leadership program.	My leadership experience has been in technology. I've overseen teams of up to 80 people, most of whom are involved in technical support/client service. And I have 5 years of experience on a nonprofit board, at MidwestYouth. Rating: M
Ten years of experience in disability services	No work experience in this area.	My interest in this role comes from my background as a family member and later guardian for my brother, a person with disabilities. I act as his guardian and have been very connected with the wide array of services available. Rating: M

Experience with fundraising, particularly a capital campaign	Some fundraising as a board member at Coats for Kids and Animal Rescue Dakotas. No capital campaigns.	I've raised funds as a board member (i.e., calling on friends, filling tables at the gala) but not at this level, and never for a capital campaign. Rating: L
Experience setting strategy; working with a board of directors	I'm on the strategy committee for my company and lead the strategic planning process. I attend and present at all board meetings. Many years of nonprofit board experience, including strategic planning.	I'm confident in my role as strategy leader, both at my company (where I have won industry awards for my approach) and at various nonprofits as a board participant in strategy. Note the strategy at Hightown Services, which was nominated for a Star Award. Rating: H

Once you have completed a Job Match Matrix for an open position, pause for a moment. Congratulate yourself. This isn't easy! Yet you've taken a crucial step to being ready to be your best in the upcoming interview.

The Four Big Topics

You're getting closer. You've investigated the hiring organization and done a deeper dive into your fit for this role. That work gives you valuable context for the interview process.

You'll next want to consider the interview itself. What will they ask you? How should you respond?

Those are important questions. Reflecting on the process itself is a valuable part of your preparation.

Every interview is different and every organization unique, but there are common themes I've seen in the thousands of interviews I've conducted and observed.

First, expect multiple probing questions and lines of inquiry in an interview. After all, the role you seek is complex and the organization's needs highly specialized. You also bring a long history and meaningful experience. There's a lot to cover.

My experience is for each hour that ticks by, you'll be asked 12 to 15 questions. Interview questions tend to fall in four thematic categories:

- Can you do this job?

- Is there a fit with our organization's values?

- How will we manage any risk factors?

- How will we work out logistics?

Not surprisingly, these questions reflect the issues the organization is likely wrestling with as they consider candidates for the position.

Let's look at each category, what it means, and how you can best prepare to address the related interview questions.

Can You Do This Job?

Almost every interview includes queries to help an organization validate that you can, indeed, do this job.

You've probably shared a resume, which has been reviewed, and possibly also participated in a telephone interview. With this input, the hiring organization has a sense of your overall skills and experience. Still, they want to make sure.

So count on questions about your background. Some general, some specific, others asking for additional details directly related to material on your resume.

Do You Fit Our Values?

Almost certainly you will get questions intended to help the interviewer discern your fit for the organization's work environment—namely, how people try to live out the organization's values. Sometimes the term "culture fit" is used, and I admit I have used that phrase myself when screening candidates. Today, I'm not terribly fond of the term "culture fit." There is something rather exclusionary about using the vague culture fit assessment to screen people, and often allows organizations to continue to bring in people who are more like them, and screen out people who are less similar. I prefer to think about seeking a person who is a "culture add" rather than a "culture fit." That allows for differences within the scope of shared values.

That said, every organization has a unique set of values, norms, and environment. You'll enjoy certain types of organizations more than others. Organizations know this and will screen for it. You, too, want to ascertain the type of place where you will do your best work. It's one thing to be able to do the job in the abstract. It's another to be able to perform effectively in a specific organizational culture.

Questions about values might address fit with the organization's mission, interest in its programs and services, stylistic fit with the work team, leadership approach, or other topics.

Be glad for these questions. Answer honestly. After all, you too want to ensure a great fit.

How Will We Manage Any Risk Factors?

An executive hire is a big commitment in organizational time, energy, and money. Interviewers will undoubtedly ask questions to ensure your hire has the greatest chance of success. They will inquire about anything that could give them pause or raise a red flag regarding your candidacy.

These might be the toughest questions you face. Interviewers might ask why you left a certain position (perhaps you were let go). They might question time gaps on your resume (perhaps you were out of work for a long time). They might wonder about your career trajectory and shift to the nonprofit world (perhaps you're running from something).

Please don't get defensive. No one is criticizing you or trying to get into your business. Your interview is simply a chance to answer anything that could be an issue.

If any question makes you feel uncomfortable or unwelcome, however, remember that you're a guest. You're under no obligation to stay in the interview if you feel the topics are inappropriate. You can, at any time, thank the interviewers for their time and excuse yourself from the meeting.

Again, most of the time, these questions are necessary and with good intent. Be honest. Be open. Be brief. If you were hiring an executive for this position, you would ask the hard questions too. Frame these questions in your mind as necessary and appropriate risk management on behalf of the hiring organization.

How Will We Work Out Logistics?

Every job has details to work out. And your interviewers might hit you with these queries in rapid succession. How much can you travel? What is your target compensation range? When can you start?

Be ready to talk about these logistical questions. They are straightforward details. Answer them as such. Don't overthink it.

Planning for the Most Common Questions

It's impossible to anticipate every possible question you'll be asked. That said,

---

There are a few questions that virtually always present themselves. Rather than tell you *how to answer* a question, I'm going to tell you *how to think* about these questions.

I never recommend planning or memorizing your interview answers. That smacks of inauthenticity and unwillingness to respond directly. How often have you been convinced by someone who arrived with a canned pitch? Have you ever been impressed by someone who regurgitates an answer to your question? I didn't think so. I've never seen this strategy work.

I repeat, no memorizing!

You're always better off answering in your own words, in the moment, in response to the exact question presented you.

So while you won't pre-plan or memorize your answers beforehand, you should be familiar with some of the most common questions.

Here are the interview questions I hear most frequently, along with tips for approaching each.

Tell us about yourself.
Almost every interview includes some version of "Tell me/us about yourself." Usually at the very beginning of an interview. An overview of your background helps kick off the rest of the discussion.

Think of this question in those terms—setting context. In other words, the question doesn't solicit an exhaustive description of every facet of your background or every job you've held. In fact, giving overly detailed answers to this question often repeats information on your resume. It doesn't add value.

Most people can comfortably give a synopsis of their background, highlighting job and career changes and major accomplishments. To make sure you are ready for this question, pretend you're asked this question, and practice giving an answer. **No memorizing! Your answer can and should be somewhat different each time.** Make sure your answer is no more than a couple of minutes long. If you're way over, consider whether you're covering too many details. Or are you getting off the main track? Did you include material that will come up in other questions?

If you've followed a corporate track, your background might not sound like the traditional experience for this job. You likely don't possess the specific content expertise (like animal welfare, arts education for seniors, or urban land development) that the role requires, but you probably have related skills and abilities.

Try to point out things in your career overview that do relate to this job. For example:

- Instead of "That experience gave me a deeper dive into the trucking industry," you might say, "That experience gave me knowledge of a completely different sector, along with the opportunity to manage a staff of 20 professionals and a department budget."

- In addition to "I was top commercial real estate producer and really learned the commercial real estate market in our city," you might add "I gained valuable community contacts and chaired our nonprofit professional organization during those years."

As you consider your career overview in response to this question, you should be overt and accurate about the career you've chosen to-date and the roles you've had. Stop short of using corporate or industry jargon that won't connect. Talk instead about things like staff size, budget size, strategic planning processes, tracking operational results, interacting with community members and stakeholders, etc. Use language that relates to your prior roles and the role you seek.

Why are you interested in our organization? In our work?

Again, you'll most certainly be asked a variation of this question. If you're coming to this role from another sector, it's almost inevitable. People want to know: Why this? Why now?

When representatives from a nonprofit ask you why you want to join their work, one answer is a no-go: "I'm mission driven."

"Marcia, why would that be?" you might think. "Don't I want to share that my interest is based on my being mission driven?"

Everyone is mission driven. Every. Single. Candidate. Ever.

Most professionals, in fact, consider themselves mission driven. While I expect that to be true of you, make your answer more nuanced than that. Heads up: A competing candidate already working in the nonprofit sector would never give such a bland answer. Besides, couldn't a thousand other jobs satisfy your objective to become more mission driven?

Saying you're mission driven isn't wrong, but you can do far better. Go deeper:

- Why specifically are you interested in this opportunity?

- What about this mission do you connect with as a person?

- How does your lived experience connect you with this work?

And consider the job itself:

- What attributes draw you to this role?

- Size? Scope? Complexity?

- Programs?

- Geographic reach?

- Clients served?

- Strong leadership team or board?

A good answer will link you and your interests to both the mission and the characteristics of this specific role.

You also don't want to say: "I want to give back."

Again, anyone applying for this job wants to give back. And the phrase "I want to give back" is about YOU. It describes what you personally want in your life and career. What about the organization and what it needs?

You aren't exactly wrong to say you're mission driven. Nor are you wrong to say at this point in your career you seek a role where you can give back. Just think and answer more holistically. Better answers make meaningful connections to the organization, the work, and the role.

What are your strengths for this position?
Most interviews include a query about your relative strengths for the job. Questions about strengths or areas of fit usually aim at your background and experience. They get at that first interview category, "Can this person do the job?"

So when you get this question, reply in terms of your background, experience, and abilities. What are you best at that is directly related to this job? What experiences have prepared you to take on these responsibilities?

In what ways—really—are you uniquely qualified for this role?
Possible items to mention:

- Years in a leadership position

- Size of budgets managed

- Number of staff

- Number of locations

- Expertise with related programs, as in operational management

- Experiences reporting to a board of directors (if applicable) and experiences serving on *related* boards

- Strategic planning experience

- Community relations experience

- Lived experience giving a unique lens into the work of the organization (i.e., you and your children were all long-time members of FFA)

What challenges might you have? What areas might be less strong? What areas might you need to develop?
If a hiring team asks about your strength areas, they're also likely to inquire about areas that aren't as strong.

Go back to your Job Match Matrix. That category you marked as low. The one that maybe pained you to admit. There's your answer. Great!

Your challenge area will likely be in content expertise. Skills like financial management, budgets, people management, strategy, operational management, and programs can be gained in many settings. They're likely strengths you would bring to a role.

**Don't be afraid to own up to your challenge areas.
They're probably points readily apparent
to the hiring organization anyway.**

If you've never worked in the field of homelessness, you probably need additional development on the specifics—like understanding causes and needs, the landscape of service providers, connections with funders, being known to others, and building relationships with partners.

Many candidates throw in the comment "But I am a fast learner!" when responding to this type of question. That might be true. However, it's more helpful to have something concrete in mind.

In an honest answer about an area or areas that require development, you might want to mention how you already are—or plan to—get up to speed in a particular area. If you are aware of a seminar (Fundraising for New Nonprofit Leaders) or a course (Understanding Nonprofit Financial Reporting) or an organization (Alliance of Arizona Nonprofits) that could help you gain skills, knowledge, and connections, mention it. Your suggestion might not be exactly how the organization would prefer to help you get that information, but it shows you're thinking about your onboarding.

What is your leadership style/communication style?

You'll almost certainly face multiple questions about your leadership style, communication style, approach to conflict, and the like. These questions get at the second category of interview questions, whether you are a culture fit for the organization.

My best advice about style questions is to gather and use as much real-life information as you can. Answers with the most merit are filled with actual information and specific examples.

Let's say you're asked this question: "What is your preferred management style?"

Your absolute worst answer will be something academic or a platitude about the topic. "I believe management is important." Or "Managers must share objectives and then support their staff."

Those answers aren't exactly wrong, but they don't illuminate anything about you.

Unfortunately, neither does your own *opinion* about what you *surmise* your management style to be. "Well, I'm pretty sure people would say I'm fair. And I bet they would say I have a good sense of humor!"

Instead, **hard data and actual feedback about your style is always best.** Think about these bits of helpful information as you prepare for interview questions about your leadership style:

- Performance appraisals: What was the direct feedback about your management style?

- 360-degree reviews: What input did you receive about your management style?

- Assessments: What do leadership style assessments say about you? Your takeaways, action points, and results?

- Executive coaching: What insights did they offer?

- Staff or peer comments: What have people said directly to you—affirming or challenging?

Answer this question with actual examples of feedback you've received, and actual words people have used.

You might get a related question about how you've grown or developed in your leadership style. Consider this carefully. Don't be afraid to share a significant leadership gap you've worked on over the years. We all have them. Be prepared to share what you did—or are doing—to enhance your capabilities in this area. What tools have you used? Who has helped you? What do you still have in front of you?

Questions about style get at whether your leadership and communication style fit in this organization. If you aren't a fit, don't you want to know it? Always be honest in answering this category of questions!

What questions do you have for us?

You probably have a truckload of questions. That's great. It would be odd if you didn't have questions in a process as important as this one.

Questions are awesome. The big issue is timing. Keep in mind, especially in initial discussions, that you may only have a few minutes for your questions as an interview winds down.

Listen for cues. An interviewer might say something like

- "We have a few minutes left. Do you have any questions?" **A few minutes.** Time for one or two questions.

- "We have time for a couple of questions." **A couple of questions.**

Take the hints embedded in interviewer questions. Ignore them at your peril.

You may have several questions, but you don't need or get to ask them all at once. Remember: The person who calls the meeting runs the meeting.

At this point, the process is all about what the hiring organization needs to know about you. Their meeting, their terms.

If you're advanced for further interviews or next steps in the hiring process, you'll have other opportunities to raise questions. If you're a finalist and it doesn't seem like you have enough time in the interviews for your questions, ask for a separate phone call or coffee to go over things.

Ask meaningful questions pertinent to the individual(s) you are meeting.

- **If you meet with board members,** for example, you might choose to ask about the organization's strategic plan or programmatic direction. You might inquire about financial health or funding sources. It would be interesting to know what they would like this new executive to accomplish in the first year.

- **If you gather with staff members,** you could ask them about the organization's culture and work environment. You might ask about what type of leadership style resonates the most with staff.

- **If you meet with peers,** you could ask about how decisions are made and how functional leaders work together. Or ask about recent successes or challenges. You might want to know what they see on the horizon that excites or worries them.

Don't try to cram more questions into the interview than time allows. Be respectful of the process.

Conversely, don't miss an opportunity to learn more and engage in meaningful discussion. Candidates who state they have no questions at all perplex the hiring team. *Doesn't this person care to learn our thoughts? They think they know 'everything'?*

What are your salary expectations?

Increasingly, nonprofits and other organizations are moving to a sticker price model where compensation for a job is set and published. It is what it is. You will get that salary whether you currently make twice that amount or half that amount. I applaud this direction.

It's easy to find out compensation amounts for leaders at most nonprofit organizations, as the information is public in the Form 990, which is readily accessed online.

If you're asked about compensation, don't get nervous. Think of it as a tactical detail that must be worked out, along with title, start date, and choice of new paint color in your office.

Do your homework. Try to learn the compensation range for this role and similar roles. ONLY apply for jobs that pay a salary comfortable for you!

Under no circumstances should you go through an interview process thinking an organization will upend its compensation range to offer you a significantly higher salary than it has paid for this job in the past.

If asked about compensation, you can say you have done research into the pay range for this job, and that you are comfortable in that range. If pressed to share your past compensation, you can do so, maybe as a range describing the last few years (i.e., "I've earned in the $105,000 to $140,000 range.") along with a statement that you are prepared to make a shift in compensation reflective of your interest in moving to a new sector.

Often the less said the better. I find that candidates frequently over-answer or over-share when it comes to pay discussions.

You might well be taking a significant pay cut. If you're fully at peace with that, it will come across. Answer graciously, honestly, and respectfully. State, "I know we'll be able to come to terms." And you likely will.

Your interviewers will ask tough questions. But this is a two-way street. Next, I'll explain how to conduct your own due diligence, asking and discovering answers for your toughest questions.

CHAPTER EIGHT

Watch Outs

Maybe you've done it. A great interview. You thought you were proceeding through a hiring process with your eyes wide open. But apparently not.

You've been so excited about a potential opportunity you neglected to see big flaws in the organization's environment. Or you've been so keen to work toward a particular organization's mission you've overlooked major problems in its financial status or even its ongoing viability.

One friend left his corner office in business for a nonprofit active in the sweet spot of his life's passions. He was familiar with the organization through pro bono work, so he assumed he had all the information he needed. His key misstep? A document presented to him as a rigorous external evaluation of the organization was actually a self-reported analysis. He arrived as an executive in a nonprofit with significant issues, and after nine maddening months, he resigned without his next position in hand.

We've talked about the importance of doing your homework. While it isn't possible to learn *everything*, you should find out as much as you can from as many sources as you can about the organization you're targeting. Learn as much as you can about the people you will be working for and with. Thoroughly familiarize yourself with the scope and responsibilities of the job itself.

No one will do your due diligence for you. Your research into the organization is as important as your efforts to win the job.

The last thing you want is to enthusiastically accept a new position only to discover a material problem that causes you regret.

Three key thoughts:

- Due diligence starts with understanding your own inclinations. Do you see flaws and respond appropriately to them—or are you quick to overlook or excuse?

- Due diligence also depends on your own humility. As you step into a new sector, acknowledge there are a thousand things you potentially don't know—and **you don't know what you don't know.**

- The further you get toward a potential role at a nonprofit, the deeper you should dig before saying yes.

Lack of information puts you in the danger zone for career mistakes.

Here are a few areas I suggest you explore as you investigate opportunities in the nonprofit sector:

Organization Due Diligence Questions

GOVERNANCE STRUCTURES	KEY FINDINGS / INFORMATION SOURCES
If you're considering a role as CEO, President or Executive Director, there will be no more important relationship than the one you have with the board of directors. You'll want to be concerned if: • The board is made up of primarily new members. (Why?) • The board giving record shows low participation in financial support of the organization. (Why?) • The board appears to be very hands-on, doing actual work in the organization. (Role clarity? Control issues?) • The board members or senior leaders do not reflect the community or clients served. (Why not? Low commitment to equity and inclusion?)	

STRATEGY	KEY FINDINGS / INFORMATION SOURCES
If you're looking at a top job in an organization, you'll need to carefully review the organization's strategic direction. You might be concerned if: • The strategy was set very recently and the job of a new leader is to carry it out. (Do you fully agree with this strategy and direction? How much flexibility is there to change or revisit a strategy recently defined? Would you rather set strategy or carry out strategy?) • The strategy is very dated. (How is the board managing the strategy of the organization? How do they track and measure success? Are they open to a new strategic plan in the near term?) • The strategic plan is flawed. (What happened? What strikes you as flawed in the plan? Can this be corrected?)	

FINANCES	KEY FINDINGS / INFORMATION SOURCES
Most nonprofits run lean operations that might feel hand-to-mouth to many people with corporate backgrounds. You might be concerned if you see: • One primary funding stream, that is, one major donor or one government contract. (What happens if this revenue stream goes away?) Personal note: I was a volunteer, years ago, at a small nonprofit that was almost entirely funded by one contract. Every few years, the organization went into a panic, worrying about possible demise if the contract were awarded elsewhere. • Unusual spending. (Any expense categories that seem strange? Is the top executive's compensation in line with other like organizations?)	

REPUTATION	KEY FINDINGS / INFORMATION SOURCES
When you join a nonprofit, you join a mission and a history. Conduct an internet search of the organization you're considering. Then search again. You might be concerned if: • There are recent reports that cast a negative light on the organization, such as financial mismanagement, poor record of service, and the like. (Can the organization recover from this?) • A recent CEO or past leadership is tainted by scandal. (Will this person be able to fundraise at a high level? Will the scandal lead to broad exits of other leaders in the organization?)	

Job Due Diligence Questions

HISTORY OF THE ROLE	KEY FINDINGS / INFORMATION SOURCES
Try to find out what has happened to people who have previously held this role. You might want to probe more if: • Several people have passed in and out of this job in recent years. (What happened? Has anything changed?) • You're following a long-term incumbent. We often see nonprofit leaders retiring after 30, 35, 40, or even 45 years in the same job. (How will the organization receive a new person in the role? How open is the organization to a new way of approaching the work?) • This is a new position, and no one has had this job. (How defined is the position? Does the role make sense to you? Is there funding for the position beyond the first year?)	

STATUS OF INCUMBENT	KEY FINDINGS / INFORMATION SOURCES
If you're following someone else in a job, it never hurts to ask where that person succeeded, what things might be enhanced, and why that individual left the organization. Be concerned if: • The person was let go and you don't like what you hear about the situation. People get fired. It happens. That doesn't mean the job is flawed or that you would not want to pursue this opportunity. But if information comes your way that makes you question the integrity of the situation, step back and evaluate. (Why are they badmouthing this person? Isn't this information confidential?) • That individual quit for another job. Again, people move on and get new jobs. Try to learn about the situation. (Does anything give you pause?) • They retired. How nice! Have they already left the organization? When is their last day? No concerns here, unless (and this is **potentially a show-stopper-level concern**) the incumbent isn't planning to leave the organization after retiring from this job. (What will they be doing? Will they report to you? Will you be peers? Have all parties really thought about this?)	

Here's a watch-out scenario more common than you might think.

Be very concerned if you hear that "Manny is retiring as Executive Director, but will stay on in the organization, still reporting to the board, doing special projects." Or "CeCe is stepping down from Chief Advancement Officer, but will stay on as a Major Gift Officer, reporting to you. We just couldn't let go of her 30 years of experience, and she just couldn't leave us either!"

Admittedly, similar scenarios can happen in business—perhaps in a family business or when an owner sells a business but hangs around as an advisor. When leaders are committed to a nonprofit cause and constituency, it's tempting to never really leave.

In case you're too eager to make your jump to a role—or too kindhearted to sense the danger—let me point out these situations are exceedingly difficult and come with a high failure rate.

At the very least, staff and stakeholders may not know how to navigate relationships with a new boss (you) even as they attempt to avoid offending their previous boss. When they have questions, they waffle between asking their previous boss, who knows an answer right away, or their new boss, who might not know the answer but who is their proper direct chain of command.

That's best case. The situation can get a whole lot worse.

If you find yourself in this situation, dig deeper. Be thoughtful and respectful. Inquire about lines of command. Ask how conflicts or discrepancies might be handled. Suggest a three- or six-month trial period for this plan. And make sure you have someone as a go-to resource you can approach if things aren't working.

Each of the areas above compel you to politely ask for further information or invite additional discussion. Some scenarios are deal-breakers where you discern a certain role or organization isn't a fit for you.

Be open.

Be gracious.

Be diligent.

CHAPTER NINE

Sticking the Landing

You've done it. Worked hard. Proven your value. Made connections that created momentum. Now you've received an offer of employment from a nonprofit organization. You're just moments from the end of your all-out effort.

Believe it or not—ready or not—you're actually making the jump. So how can you avoid stumbling at the last moment—and stick your landing?

Understanding the Offer

You're probably accustomed to settings where virtually all job offers have room for negotiation. That might not be the case with an offer from a nonprofit.

I can't think of many nonprofits that engage in the wheeling-dealing-we'll-do-whatever-it-takes negotiations of some business settings.

For nonprofits that do engage in negotiation, the points of conversation are fewer and the range of movement smaller.

That should be your mental starting point. In all my experiences recruiting across the for-profit and nonprofit sectors, a very limited negotiation is simply reality in nonprofit.

Start there. Then work through these next steps:

- Like any other offer of employment, ask for the offer in writing.

- Read the offer letter thoroughly. Note details. Start date. Title. Compensation. Benefits and perquisites. Contingencies. How does this align with your understanding?

- You've known all along that nonprofit compensation and benefits packages will likely be less than you've earned in another sector—in many cases quite a lot less. You now have an offer of employment and you see a number. It's indeed lower than you've earned before. This might be the moment that tests you.

Should you negotiate for a higher compensation? I can honestly say I've worked with many corporate executives who, despite affirming their interest in the nonprofit sector and their comfort with a lower compensation range, turn into negotiating machines once presented with an offer. It's disconcerting to see these individuals bring corporate-level compensation numbers into the picture.

A high percentage of nonprofit organizations publish the compensation for a role right from the beginning.

Actually, in all sectors, the days of clandestine discussions about pay followed by job offers containing a proposed salary based on your historical pay are increasingly a thing of the past. That tradition has led to pervasive and systemic underpayment of women and people of color. It is wrong. The nonprofit sector has led the way toward pay equity. As such, you'll find many situations of a set salary amount planned and prearranged before the job opportunity is even launched. It might be written into the Job Description or Position Profile.

You and the organization have probably already discussed compensation. Unless the offer is different from a published number, or what you learned in previous conversations, you may have little room to negotiate.

If a compensation range has been shared with you, and the offer is lower in the range, you might be able to request a small adjustment. But remember you signed up for this. You'll likely need training and support to get up to speed in the position. Are you truly worth what the previous executive—who has years of sector experience—is worth? What do *you* think is the best way for this nonprofit to use its resources—more pay for you? When you've hired people, have you offered top range for someone with little experience doing the exact type of work?

The benefits package will probably be less comprehensive. You may have to contribute significantly more for the employee-paid portion of your health insurance costs.

Again, you knew this. Now that the numbers are real and in front of you, can you be okay with this?

If aspects of the offer remain unclear, it's never wrong to ask for a brief conversation to clarify particulars. If the offer changes, it might make sense to request an updated offer letter.

Still enthusiastic? Great. Starting to rethink? That's crucial to admit to yourself.

It's time to get real. Take it all in. Make your decision.

Saying NO

If you have significant reservations you can't resolve, don't accept the offer. However, you should also be prepared to do some soul searching.

- Was it something specific about this offer that falls short?

- Will other organizations and offers likely be different?

- Does your reaction give you pause about the whole notion of moving into the nonprofit sector?

If you don't accept this offer, take a breather. Reflect. Regroup. Consider how to move ahead with similar positions or perhaps to take a different path.

Senior financial executive Carri, for example, was committed to obtaining a new role in a nonprofit organization focused on economic development in urban settings. She networked. She attended nonprofit leadership training. She became familiar with the landscape of providers in economic development services. When she received an offer to become a Director within the Small Business Administration in her city, she was initially excited.

However, something didn't feel right. Carri reviewed the offer. She thought she had been prepared to take a smaller pay package. Truthfully, she wasn't. Rather than enter a protracted negotiation Carri felt would be unfair to the nonprofit, she declined the offer.

Carri knew she was probably burning a bridge with the organization, and she didn't want to set herself up for a situation where that could happen again. She looked inward and realized a full-time job at a nonprofit probably wasn't the right path. Carri decided to take an equally meaningful career turn in another direction.

Getting to YES

Are you ready to say yes? Great! But before you do, pause. Doublecheck.

You're undertaking a major shift in both work and life. It's a big deal when you accept. You want to be 100% sure this is the right decision for you.

How to do that?

- **Check your gut.** What are you feeling? Are you excited about all aspects of this job—the work activities, the organizational mission, the leadership team, and other staff who will partner with you during this next season of work? Do you have reservations? What are your hesitations? Are they the natural uncertainties that come from moving into a new job or something more?

- **Check with trusted advisors.** What do your closest family and friends think? Do they support this opportunity? Do they harbor objections or misgivings about you moving ahead? Hopefully, you've had these conversations along the way, and now that the offer is real, you'll receive resounding support.

- **Think through the logistics.** You've already considered aspects such as work hours, compensation, and the like. Any lingering concerns?

If you think you're ready to sign on the dotted line, please do something: Think about it one last time!

Saying YES!

Ready? Fantastic. Accept the offer enthusiastically!

Wesley was a construction supervisor, who, after 20 years in the business, began feeling restless. Many years as a caregiver for his father had given him a passion for serving older adults, and he noticed a steady transformation within himself. After his father died, Wesley wondered if he could apply his personal experience with caregiving and his supervisory and budgeting expertise to something different.

Fast forward several months, Wesley looks down at his laptop to a fresh message from the President of a long-term care provider. The subject line: *Offer Letter Attached.*

Smiling, Wesley opens the document. The contents are what he expected. A salary about half of what he made in his previous role—yikes! But a list of responsibilities that truly energized him—yahoo! He also knew the move would make his father proud.

Wesley couldn't wait to tell his husband. The next day, he sent an email returning the offer letter, signed, to his new employer. The subject line: *Offer Accepted!*

Once you accept an offer, you have plenty of people to thank. Share your gratitude and excitement with the representatives of the nonprofit organization, including the individual(s) you will report to. Let them know how happy you are. Say out loud how eager you are to join them and make an impact.

In the days before you step into your new role, don't forget to circle back and thank everyone who helped you get there. As soon as you're able to share the news, send a message of gratitude to those who were part of your journey. Include your updated contact information so you can stay in touch. Offer to be helpful to your contacts in the future.

Then, sit back and smile.
You did it.

You're full of hope and expectations.
You'll soon make that real-life jump to a nonprofit!

What Happens After You Accept?

After you accept the offer and begin planning for your new role, you'll undoubtedly reflect on the journey that brought you to this point. Well, that's not *all* you're thinking. Plenty of other thoughts are likely racing through your mind.

I know this is a big deal. One of life's epic moments.

Some leaders have told me about positive, uplifting emotions that struck when they heard the good news.

- Randy learned in a voicemail that he was receiving an offer to join a small nonprofit providing English Language Learning programs for adults. His first reaction? **He anticipated the joy he would experience sharing the news with family and close friends.** After all, this tight group had provided him with love and support through a journey of several months.

- **Noya wiped away tears of happiness.** A two-year process of discernment and activities—many outside of her comfort zone—led to this moment. She often held her emotions inside during the long search process, not wanting her fears to derail her. Now she let it all out.

Noya realized her feelings weren't unique to landing a nonprofit job and could be the reaction of anyone landing any job after extended unemployment. But she had been through several job searches. This experience was uniquely intense because she started with few contacts in the nonprofit world, and she was learning about the sector even as she sought to make the case for her readiness to join it.

- **Shoshana's first reaction was to think of her children and young grandson.** She visualized them many years in the future, reflecting on her life. She could almost hear a discussion taking place after she is gone, with her children telling the story of her work with immigrant communities. Shoshana believes her career shift will communicate a message to her family beyond what any words could do.

- **Kim was thrilled beyond belief.** After a career working to increase shareholder value for people he would never meet, he would finally have an inspirational answer to the pesky question, "What motivates you to get out of bed in the morning?" An extrovert with a broad set of acquaintances, Kim immediately thought about how much he looked forward to answering questions about his work and his career interests.

- **Rhonda hung up the phone and fell into her office chair in silent reflection.** Chosen as the new Executive Director of a social services nonprofit that had provided services and information to her family years ago, Rhonda had always promised herself she would give back. And this coming Monday, she would live out the story she began writing for herself many years ago. She described the feeling as "coming full circle."

There is, however, another side. Other leaders have confided to me that along with the positive sentiments, they also experienced unexpected reactions.

- **Cissy had "the good feels" about her offer. She also felt doubt.** Soon to become the administrative manager at a nonprofit organization providing funding and education for childcare providers, her second thoughts weren't about the role or the logistics. Cissy had long factored in the pay cut and potentially long hours of nonprofit work. Her family supported her, and she was all-in.

Still, it's one thing to consider these things in the abstract and another to see them in print in a formal offer. Her intent was being tested. Was she *really* sure? Cissy determined she was. Her doubts were fleeting, all things considered, but she wisely acknowledged and dealt with them.

- **Rodrigo dreaded telling his current employer he would be leaving the company.** He was taking a job with an organization providing street outreach and support services for individuals experiencing homelessness, knowing his managers had invested in him and put him on the promotional fast track. His decision would be seen as betrayal. But he also knew his heart was no longer in the work. He hoped his bosses would understand promoting someone else would be better for the company. At least in the long run.

From extreme excitement to pangs of doubt, you might experience these same reactions as you reach the end of your job search. It's okay. You're acknowledging change. And figuring out how to deal with it.

Change is good. It's time to ensure your change is successful.

Getting Off to a Good Start

You explored your nonprofit inklings and landed a nonprofit role. Perhaps you conducted extensive networking meetings. Maybe you spent significant time familiarizing yourself with your local nonprofit market. You might have taken courses or seminars to enhance your skills.

**Getting that offer is a huge deal.
Congratulations and welcome aboard!
And yet the offer is just the beginning.**

You hope and expect to make a positive impact in your new role. Let's look at some of the things you should do to assure a strong start that leads to long-term success.

Things You'll Need to Know

During the hiring process, you no doubt learned more than you ever expected about the organization you're joining. Superb! There's likely, however, so much more you'll need as you start your role.

No matter your job or where it fits in the organization, you have a lot to learn.

Don't assume the information conveyed in your research and interviews was exhaustive or even adequate for getting underway.

A recently hired nonprofit executive I worked with got off to a rocky start by not taking time to ground himself in the organization's history and up-to-the-moment status. When he began talking future ideas, he was perceived as insensitive and ill-prepared without thorough knowledge and empathy for the past and present.

Do a double- and triple-check. Each job presents different requirements for your early days and weeks, but most nonprofit positions share common elements. If you aren't well-versed in the following topics, put these items on your to-do list for your first 30 days. Indeed, look for opportunities to dive into parts of these activities even before Day One.

- **Objectives and Expectations.** As an entrant from the corporate world, this job is likely significantly different from anything you've ever done. **So much so that I feel both excitement and trepidation for you!** Although you might have learned much in your interviews and might possess a written job description, don't, however, leave to chance a formal understanding of goals and objectives.

Request whatever the organization has for job descriptions, position profiles, performance dashboards, and the like. Request a session with your boss—or board chair, if you are an Executive Director or CEO—to map out expectations for your first six months and first year.

Discuss how your performance will be measured. Who will provide input about your performance? How often? Who will share the information with you?

• **Financial Information.** Nonprofits are required to file a Form 990 with the IRS and their state attorney general. This is a long and complicated form, but it's valuable for you to grapple with the information your new organization must submit annually.

Additionally, in most roles you'll want to learn the types of income your new organization relies on and if sources have changed over the years. If a charitable nonprofit, how much is contributed (donated) income versus earned (fee for service) income? Of the contributed income, how much is institutional funding and how much comes from individuals? Is your organization happy with the ratios? If an association nonprofit, what is the split between dues and non-dues revenue?

Finally, ask for a copy of the most recent budget, balance sheet, and profit and loss documents—paying special attention to your area of the organization.

• **Strategic Plans.** Wherever your new role sits in the organization, overarching goals matter to your work. There's probably a formal strategy, and if there isn't a current strategic plan, there's likely an annual operating plan. Learn how the ideas were developed, who contributed, how goals and targets were determined, and most importantly how your own work supports the big plan.

- **Programmatic Information.** Just as the organization has an overall budget, there may be separate budgets for each of its programs. Are the programs delivered through staff alone or do they rely on a large volunteer base? How does the organization recruit, recognize, and maintain relationships with its volunteers?

Relationships You'll Need to Build

In your job search, you saw the amazing power of relationships. Those bonds will continue to be powerful and valuable to you. Your first days on the job will require you to consider how you initiate and enhance key relationships.

Before you start your new position, circle back to everyone who helped you along the way. Don't forget the relationships that got you to this point. Who met with you? Who took your call? Who responded to an email? Who gave you advice? Share your good news along with your new professional contact information. Do this right away.

Your early tenure in your new organization is prime time to connect:

- **Internal Relationships. If you report to an Executive Director or CEO,** this relationship is paramount. Meet with your boss right away. What are expectations for your first week? Month? What activities will be most important? What support will your boss provide?

  If you report directly to a board of directors, consider this group your boss, especially the Executive Committee of the board. Meet as soon as possible with the board chair. Ask the same questions. What are the expectations for your early weeks and months on the job? What activities are critical? Are there any burning issues? What would the board like to have addressed right away?

  If you have a direct staff, you'll also want to meet with them right away. Perhaps you can meet your staff as a group in a less formal meet and greet. As soon as you can, however, schedule one-on-one sessions with each. What do they want in a new boss? What's going well? What challenges do they face? What do they celebrate? What keeps them up at night? How can you help right away? How would they like to work with you?

If you have a large staff, solicit input from others on how to best communicate with them. No doubt, an organizational announcement has gone out about your hire. Others may help you decide how best to reach out to the full staff. An email blast? An e-newsletter? A big tent session?

- **External Relationships.** The nature of your new role will dictate the external relationships important to cultivate. These could include funders (government, philanthropic, individual donors), elected officials, or journalists. Your organization might have partner organizations with key contacts.

Look for professional groups related to your new work and sector. Ask around about how your organization participates in these. Be as active as possible in the nonprofit community, both to make valuable connections and to continue learning.

Plans You'll Need to Make

I've encouraged you to gather information. Now turn that data into action. Capture your plans for immediate activities in a detailed 30- 60- 90-Day Plan. There are numerous books, blogs, and other resources available online or in bookstores on how to write your onboarding plan. I like *The First 90 Days: Proven Strategies for Getting Up to Speed Faster and Smarter* by Michael D. Watkins. Leverage these resources along with anything your organization provides you to prepare a detailed activity scheme for your first few months on the job.

- **Your Onboarding Plan.** I love the idea of creating a formal plan to pull together what you need to learn and who you need to know to start well.

This could include checklists building on items I've mentioned. Perhaps your plan looks like a grid, with segments for Before Start Date, First Week, First Month, Second Month, and so on. You might have bulleted activities in each column.

After you create your plan, invite others—boss, peers, mentor—to look at your notes and weigh in. What have you missed? What priorities might they rearrange?

Before you get too far, see if your organization already has onboarding plans for staff. A recent nonprofit client was so excited to welcome their CEO that the senior staff and a couple of board members created a detailed onboarding plan for the new leader before they were even selected. If you're fortunate enough to have your organization design a plan, augment those activities with other items above.

- **A Development Plan.** This is separate from your onboarding plan. It's not about settling into the job but rather getting better at the job. After all, you've built a track record of accomplishments and valuable skills. Those helped secure you a spot in a nonprofit organization. What will keep you a strong contributor? What will assure you remain relevant to the organization over time?

With your boss, board members, mentor, or coach, think about areas you wish to continue to develop, and set a plan. These plans are usually set and measured annually, but you can be flexible. The key is that you set up intentional activities to keep your skills sharp.

Don't Stop Now!

You will change. Your organization will morph. Community or population needs are constantly shifting. Funding sources will come and go.

I'd like to think a year or two after starting your new role at a nonprofit organization, you're thriving as a prized employee at your organization and a valued member of the larger sector. What does that look like? You're active! You join and contribute to industry associations. Attend relevant seminars, in-person or online. Read topical journals and blogs. Follow thought leaders. Subscribe to daily information emails from helpful sources. Network with fellow nonprofit leaders.

And most importantly? With the same intent and energy that got you this far, you're pressing on to create impact in new ways.

CHAPTER TEN

Ten Ways to Make the Jump

This might be the most important chapter in this book.

Why? Because it contains a message absolutely essential for making your jump to the nonprofit world. The transition from for-profit to nonprofit is rarely simple. It's most often lengthy. So what do you do in the meantime? What if your plans don't come together as you expect? And if your goal remains a full-time permanent position in the nonprofit of your dreams, how do you press on?

If you're willing to reflect on your situation, stretch your thinking, and potentially adapt to new plans, there's always a path forward. Know this with certainty:

There are...

many ways for you to do nonprofit work
myriad roles where you can be mission driven
countless approaches to serving others and bettering your world.

I mentioned early in this book that 90 percent of the business professionals who contact me about a move to the nonprofit sector have a singular objective—to become Executive Director or President of a nonprofit organization. That's a problem. Most of these folks aren't prepared for those roles, and there simply aren't many available jobs at that level.

That's the bad news. The good news is the point of this chapter. There are many ways to contribute.

You can ALWAYS find opportunities to actively help others and create impact in the near- and long-term. In this chapter, I'll spell out 10 scenarios for you to consider as possibilities for your jump.

So don't skip any of these stories. This is your life, and these are crucial decisions. I want to give you LOTS to ponder!

Make the Jump 1: Reframe

Keep everything the same. And change it up!

WHAT THIS MEANS: Sometimes the best strategy is to stay put—and reaffirm, reengage, and reimagine where you are.

It's always wise to take a long, thoughtful look at your present setting before deciding to move on. Even if you've been longing for a change for what feels like forever, rethink. Just as you need to do your due diligence on any new job, give your current situation the same critical examination, especially upsides you might be discounting.

As you consider a job transition, what thoughts and emotions drive you? Have you allowed time to make wise and planful determinations about your direction? Have you sought counsel? Is your movement toward a nonprofit a *pull* to what you want or a *push*—a reaction—to a circumstance or event such as a new boss, altered job responsibilities, missing a promotion, or what?

Think hard about finding joy and meaning where you're at. Can you reenlist with the mission of your company? Acknowledge ways you're already creating impact, like coaching and mentoring others? Can you become that sought-after boss who provides professional development to your team—and beyond? Think about creating a positive workplace culture for your department or function. These are all meaningful ways of giving back.

WHAT YOU'LL NEED: Maybe nothing. Or a variety of resources.

You might discern you need a dose of professional development. How could a coach help you enhance your supervisory skills? What leadership training courses or certifications are available? Could you join an executive roundtable to meet regularly with other leaders?

You might also need an attitude adjustment. Once upon a time, I sure did. Years ago, I felt unhappy and stuck in my career in executive search. I sought out a coach, who advised me "not to leave my profession but to leave my bad attitude about my profession." That stung! It was honest and accurate. But what a helpful insight! Could a coaching conversation with a professional, a colleague, or other trusted advisor be useful to you? They might point out what you can't see for yourself.

SOMEONE WHO DID THIS: Jeff was a sales representative in the hospital supply industry. Well-regarded by peers, he led his organization's diversity committee as well as its local college recruiting. After continually far exceeding his quota, Jeff hit a year where he was among his division's lowest performers. He attributed his downturn partly to burnout and partly to a redesign of company territories. His new assignment siphoned off his favorite clients and added others where he had no history. Multiply those factors by the normal exhaustion of having two small children at home, and Jeff lacked the energy necessary to build new relationships.

When Jeff called me, he was ready to take a job as the youth director at his faith community, a role that had impacted him as a teenager and where he felt he could take a break from the territory changes. He and his spouse felt they could cut back to make the finances work, although that reality was a lingering question.

I encouraged Jeff to step back and reflect. I suggested he meet with a job transition coach to discuss the pros and cons of staying vs. leaving. He asked the church for more time to discern his direction.

Jeff and his coach created strategies for him to reengage in his job. He asked his boss if he could stay in touch with former clients, and he received a go-ahead, allowing him to maintain important relationships. He also recognized afresh how much it meant to him to contribute company-wide to diversity and college recruiting.

Ultimately, Jeff decided to stay put for a couple more years. He and his wife began a more aggressive savings program so he could more easily make a jump in the future if opportunity and desire aligned.

Make the Jump 2: Philanthropy

Accumulate wealth and give it away.

WHAT THIS MEANS: You forgo a job in a nonprofit, but you spend your time investigating, evaluating, and financially supporting one or more causes or organizations. You become a philanthropist.

You will likely define a target:

- a giving **area**, perhaps your local geography, or

- a giving **direction**, such as sexual violence and domestic abuse prevention

You can work alone or with others to discover and vet organizations serving in these areas. Your major gifts to selected organizations could be one-time or recurring. You might want to get to know the management staff of these organizations, and in turn you might be asked for input.

WHAT YOU'LL NEED: Money!

How much money you need depends on the size of the gifts (grants) you want to make and whether you intend your grantmaking organization to exist in perpetuity or be drawn down over a predetermined number of years. In any case, you'll need substantial money. Experts suggest a minimum of $500,000 to make setting up a philanthropy worth the cost.

You'll also require legal and financial assistance to set up your philanthropic/grantmaking organization. Advisors will help you create the structure of the organization and consider various granting mechanisms.

You may also involve others—family members, for example—as a sounding board or formal board of directors. You may choose to affiliate with a community foundation.

Philanthropy takes more than money. Really important? A spirit of learning. This jump into the nonprofit world requires investigating and selecting organizations whose goals and results most connect with your own mission.

- How will you choose nonprofit organizations that best meet your criteria?

- What exactly are your criteria?

- Will you give one-time gifts for special programs or ongoing gifts to support general operating costs?

- What's the lifespan of your giving?

People who work in the field of philanthropy are consummate learners. They constantly add to their knowledge of the nonprofit field.

- Who is doing what?

- Where are the best practices?

- What could really make a difference, if it only had a bit more support?

- How will I assess whether my contributions are being used as I intended?

- Will I require significant reporting of results—even if the reporting takes resources away from programs?

There's much to consider. You'll probably want to create a network of individuals with similar interests, and philanthropic partners with whom you can convene to share learnings and best practices. You might want to participate in a philanthropic member organization.

SOMEONE WHO DID THIS: I met Wendy, a world-traveling marketing executive, a couple years ago. She was keen to join a nonprofit organization, in part to lessen her heavy travel schedule. Years as a road warrior for a Fortune 500 manufacturer had become wearing.

Wendy connected with me because she wanted to explore moving to a career more connected with her desire to make a positive change in the world. And she wanted to get off the road!

An avid outdoorsperson, Wendy's strongest interests related to wildlife, particularly endangered species. Her international travel exposed her to the breadth of the natural world firsthand. Wendy wanted to make a difference for animals.

Wendy felt hesitant asking about nonprofit job opportunities. Intense travel left her with little time to volunteer. She had virtually no experience with nonprofits—and she knew it.

She also wondered how much she could earn, even in a leadership role. "How much do you earn now?" I asked. "A bit over $750,000 per year," she answered. I gulped. "Well, let's talk about some alternatives."

I followed up by asking Wendy if she felt comfortable discussing her investment portfolio. Had she ever thought about philanthropy as a next career step? The more we talked, the more excited she got.

It took a couple years for Wendy to exit her high-flying, high-paying job to start a foundation named after her father, the person who instilled a love of nature in her. Wendy's philanthropic activities let her learn about and support organizations that speak to her core purpose. "My heart sings!" she later shared.

Wendy now maintains an assortment of challenging and interesting activities. She's perpetually studying programs, meeting people, and acquiring knowledge about organizations in her area of focus. She's becoming a thought leader, attending several wildlife conservation conventions and accepting an invitation to speak at a wildlife conference next year.

Make the Jump 3: Add On

Add meaningful, regular volunteer experiences to your life.

WHAT THIS MEANS: Consider this intriguing question:

- Can you envision yourself fully satisfying your desire to give back through something other than a full-time nonprofit job?

Embedded in that question is another:

- Will you feel the same type of fulfillment working for free as performing a job for pay?

And one more:

- Many volunteer jobs are likely less strategic, less high level. Would that be a problem for you?

If you're in a full-time business role and you wonder about quitting to pursue a nonprofit job, what about keeping your job and adding volunteering? By serving the community in a volunteer role, you might feel better about your corporate job. Volunteerism, added to your day job, could increase your contentment quotient. You can enjoy the benefits of your business career while adding new and gratifying pieces to your life through volunteerism.

If you think you're interested in the nonprofit sector but aren't entirely sure, volunteer roles could be the best way for you to discern if you could engage in the work full-time.

If you're retired but seeking to return to work, volunteer gigs might be a way to go. Volunteer engagements, carefully selected, could make for a rich collective offering both fulfillment and flexibility.

Volunteer opportunities in nonprofits will be as varied as the sector itself. You could spend time each week mucking the barn at a stable providing horse riding experiences for individuals with disabilities, or you could become board chair of your region's largest social service organization. What types of volunteer service resonate with you?

Consider your situation and your available time. How often could you volunteer—daily, weekly, monthly? And how much—large blocks of time or short periods of occasional availability?

WHAT YOU'LL NEED: Clarity and opportunity.

First, dialog honestly with yourself about the kinds of volunteer engagements that fit you. Would you fill almost any gap for the right cause, or do you prioritize serving in board or governance capacities? Perhaps both? Will you be okay with a non-glamorous volunteer role? How would you feel telling friends and family about these activities? How will they react?

You might personally love reading books to kids at the public library, but will you wish you were instead the head librarian? Will you proudly tell your neighbors you walk dogs and sit cats at the local Humane Society? I hope so, but please think deeply about whether these types of roles would have perceived reputational consequences for you.

You'll also need to search out the right opportunities. Your discoveries might come through your network, not unlike reaching out if you were looking for a full-time job. This would be particularly true of a nonprofit board assignment. Or you might find a role through social media posts or online sites that catalog opportunities for nonprofit involvement.

Check your local paper and community websites. It's worth a look. My own local paper, for example, lists opportunities for everything from assisting at ELL classes to making sandwiches at a shelter to organizing a linen drive to providing transportation to cancer patients.

Not to your taste? The listing also included opportunities to assist all summer at a zoo camp program or coach teenage girls using an activity-based curriculum of running and exercise. There was a post as volunteer receptionist and one to get trained as a volunteer donor relations assistant. And that was just this week!

SOMEONE WHO DID THIS: Alta works in management in the telecommunications industry, enjoying a highly successful career. Alta and I were peers in the training department of a tech company long ago, and we've stayed in touch ever since.

Besides being a capable supervisor and whip smart technical advisor, Alta has a creative side. Mostly, she loves to sew. I've seen Alta create beautiful clothing and home accessories for friends, relatives, and herself. I'm always amazed at her level of detail as well as the beautiful results.

Alta often told me she wished she could quit her job and do something more meaningful. We brainstormed what that could look like. Each time we thought of a possible role in the nonprofit sector, it made Alta reflect on the positive attributes in her current job.

Ultimately, the right situation found her. Alta's church put out a call for individuals to volunteer with a faith community in Puerto Rico that was partnering with a new initiative in the rural part of the country. In particular, the initiative was around helping women who had traditionally worked in farming recover from the economic devastation of natural disaster by teaching them the skill of sewing. These women could then obtain work and provide for their families.

When Alta heard of this, it sounded almost too good to be true. Upon learning more, she was even more enthralled by the idea. This volunteer engagement required travel to Puerto Rico every quarter (no problem, Alta had accumulated significant paid time off) and weekly videoconferencing and telephone calls with the women's group leaders in Puerto Rico.

Alta kept her job at the telecommunications firm, at least for a couple of years; she recently announced her retirement. And her role with the women's sewing cooperative both lifted her spirits and taught her much about working in the nonprofit sector, specifically in international economic development and women's economic development. Further, it made her feel more fulfilled at the telecommunications firm. The combination of her existing job and the volunteer role was perfect, especially as she learned and developed her skills at the nonprofit. Alta will soon retire from her business career, but she will not retire altogether. She'll continue her work with the sewing cooperative. And she has added a second volunteer engagement teaching sewing skills to immigrant women in her own area. The last I checked, Alta feels fulfilled and gratified, as she has throughout most of her career.

Make the Jump 4: Business with a Purpose

Find a mission that resonates with you.

WHAT THIS MEANS: My belief behind this jump strategy is that there isn't an either-or between the for-profit and nonprofit sectors. One isn't "all about profit" and the other "all about mission." Indeed, many businesses carry out incredibly meaningful work. Further, some nonprofits struggle to perform against their mission.

There's an idea that drives many of the businesspeople who ask me for advice about a potential jump. Typically, the grind of a difficult culture or a significant triggering event makes the caller question their organization's values and mission. The person then transfers those concerns to the entire for-profit sector.

Many advice-seekers believe the issues that frustrate them about their current job—unethical dealings, questionable decisions, high pressure—must be common to the business sector.

To escape, they conclude they must leave corporate life altogether.

I understand the angst behind that line of thinking, but I don't think the reasoning is sound. Listening to the backstories of thousands of job candidates tells me that many if not most businesses seek to operate with ethics and integrity. I've worked for several myself. **The trick is finding a place to call home.**

Before assuming a nonprofit organization is the only place to live out your values, consider seeking out businesses that share and operate under those same priorities.

WHAT YOU'LL NEED: You'll need to clarify your values and consider how you can best live them out at work.

I'm a proponent of choosing a positive view. Instead of focusing on what you *don't* want or what's *wrong* at an employer, think about what you *do* want. Start by identifying your core values:

- What's important to you?

- What types of values would you connect with most in the workplace?

- How would this look?

Think also about mission:

- What organizational missions do you most resonate with? Like health care for women. Feeding people with organic products. Making railroad transportation safe.

- If you could work for a business with this mission, how would you rate your likely satisfaction? What are the upsides and downsides?

You'll again need to use your best investigative abilities to find potential opportunities with a mission and values match. Approach your network.

Talk to trusted advisors, peers, and thought leaders. Share your interest in connecting with organizations that share your values. Share your commitment to working with an organization whose mission is exciting and meaningful for you.

Poke around and see what you find.

What do you discover? Big companies? Small family-owned firms? What's out there? Can you satisfy your desire to live out your values without exiting the for-profit sector?

SOMEONE WHO DID THIS: Bree (they/them) contacted me several times, starting with their resume and a note about their interest in moving to a nonprofit.

A few months later, they reached back to reiterate their interest in the nonprofit space. We didn't have any assignments that were a fit for Bree, but that didn't slow their search.

Bree was working their network, and I often heard their name come up. With a good sense of their own career strengths (communications) and their core values (transparency, diversity, and collaboration), they were actively learning about regional organizations where they could find that elusive fit.

Over the course of a year, Bree continued to check in. Recently, they called to say they had obtained a new position. I was a bit surprised they had joined a large medical device manufacturing firm—not a nonprofit! Bree, however, related that they felt they had accomplished their objective of finding a match in mission and values. The company they joined is known for its commitment to important work. They joined a division led by an outstanding individual who actively develops the team.

With a clear sense of the values-based culture they were seeking, Bree was able to compare those against the division's employee engagement scores—some of the highest results I'd ever heard.

I congratulated Bree. They knew what mattered to them, could articulate it, and found a terrific match.

Make the Jump 5: Interim Assignments

Take your expertise from place to place.

WHAT THIS MEANS: Taking on limited-term assignments at nonprofit organizations.

Nonprofits often hire interims to fill senior leadership spots as well temporary assignments in roles including accounting, human resources, fundraising, and IT.

For example, organizations frequently need Interim Executive Directors to staff the top position during a time of change. The previous leader perhaps left unexpectedly for a new job. Or no successor was found prior to a planned retirement. Sometimes the organization deliberately creates space with an interim during a realignment and search.

Other interim opportunities open when a nonprofit needs limited-time specialized assistance, such as during a food shelf inventory, membership drive, or recruitment season for dozens or more camp counselors.

Whatever the case, you can bring your skills and abilities into the nonprofit organization for a timed project, typically three to six months.

I know several leaders who thrive on interim assignments and have built a career out of this work. They all have a unique ability to quickly embed themselves in an organization during a transition or other challenges. If needed, they can make significant changes—or hold down the fort until a permanent leader arrives. They can assess staff and programs and perhaps assist with board development and governance. The interim leaders I know are always in high demand!

WHAT YOU'LL NEED: Intentionality about whether an interim assignment is right for you.

- Do non-permanent roles pique your interest?

- How do you feel about on and off work with periods of downtime between?

- What kinds of temporary assignments have you undertaken in the past?

- Did you like the dynamic of short-term gigs?

- Would you be able to really grab hold of the job but let go at the right time?

You'll need to be straightforward and open about your interest in considering interim work. Create business cards. Set up a website. Join a lead-sharing group. If you think interim work might be for you, tell your network. Explain that you're open to interim assignments and be specific about the variety of opportunities that would be a fit.

If you haven't been an interim leader in the past, connect with others who have. Figure out what makes them tick. Ask about what made them successful. What to focus on? What to watch out for? Read and discover all you can about being an interim leader.

Interim leadership is a distinct specialization for leaders with the right technical and organizational skills.

You'll obviously learn a ton about the nonprofit sector by serving as an interim. But that's not a reason to pursue these roles. Don't take on an interim position just to educate yourself about the sector. Only take on interim roles where you feel 100 percent comfortable with the responsibilities.

Even with thorough due diligence, interim leaders say there's always far more to an assignment than what was presented.

More complexity. More financial difficulty. More staff problems. More legal issues. You name it! That might be the challenge you're looking for—or not!

Along with skills that fit the assignment, you also need to show up with a spirit of positivity. As an interim, you'll discover plenty about what isn't going well. Your role isn't about finding fault or placing blame. It's about problem-solving and using your expertise to help bridge a gap in a key role.

Do you have what it takes to provide relief and invest heavily in an organization—all while knowing your time will come to an end? How will you make that case to a hiring team?

SOMEONE WHO DID THIS: I met Malcolm at a conference for board members of professional and member associations. We were both attending a session on board governance.

Malcolm had spent most of his career as a Director of Information Technology in a variety of sectors, at the time as a Director of Data Science and Analytics at a very large law firm. He was currently chair of a regional chamber of commerce, his fourth round on the board of a member association. Clearly, he loved that type of group! As we left the conference, we agreed to stay in touch.

Malcom was growing interested in making a shift from corporate into the nonprofit sector, specifically to a trade group or member organization.

As active and well-connected as Malcolm was in professional association and member organization circles, offers for permanent full-time employment eluded him. We talked a few times during the frustrating months he spent applying and interviewing unsuccessfully for various openings.

Malcolm sought feedback and was told he was pleasant and gracious in interviews. His many years of relevant board experiences counted for a lot. Still, his career in technology leadership gave hiring executives pause. His overall experience made his candidacy feel unproven compared to other candidates.

At the same time this was going on, Malcolm had the opportunity to serve on a committee at his faith community. The committee was tasked with the selection of a senior faith leader to fill in for a few months while the incumbent leader took medical leave. Malcolm and his fellow committee members talked with candidates with expertise in interim capacities.

That got Malcolm thinking. His experience in technology was largely project-based. Frankly, he loved it. He was exceptional at coming into new situations and assessing situations and teams. He could move quickly or slowly as needed. With his deep experience of board service with multiple organizations, he had a sense of the multitude of issues that could be out there.

Soon, with a fresh objective and new business cards, Malcolm sought out opportunities for interim work in his target sector. He soon landed a four-month project running a trade association for professionals in the aftermarket automotive parts industry. It went so well that after two months, the board chair asked Malcolm if he was interested in taking the job permanently. Malcolm declined. He was already starting to get calls about other interim assignments, and he was excited about his new niche.

Make the Jump 6: Consulting

Spread your expertise.

WHAT THIS MEANS: Most organizations use capable consultants to provide services from strategic planning to audits to database management. Nonprofit organizations are no different. Rather than seek one full-time job, you can deploy your skills providing consulting services independently or in league with a consulting firm.

WHAT YOU'LL NEED: As with the role of interim executive, be intentional about developing a consultancy. Don't consider consulting as a hedge against finding a full-time job. It isn't fair to your potential consulting clients.

If you intend to create your own practice as a solo consultant, you'll need all the tools and planning of jumpstarting any small business.

You'll need a website, business materials, the whole shebang. There are plenty of resources to help you do this. Use all you can.

Start by meeting with several trusted advisors to get input and advice about where nonprofits might value your specific skills and experiences in a consulting role. Try too to meet with nonprofit organizations. Would any give you your first assignment? Perhaps discounted or pro bono?

As a consultant, you'll spend a significant amount of time—the bulk of your hours at first—drumming up business. How will you go about this?

A variety of approaches could be effective: Social media promotion? Presentations about your subject matter? Wining and dining potential clients? In my own executive search practice, one of our best sources of referrals is other executive search firms, or companies that provide similar services. We refer business when we're overloaded or when an assignment better suits another practice.

To succeed as a consultant, you need deep knowledge not only of the nonprofit landscape but of competing nonprofit consultants. Who's out there? What are their practice specialties? Would your business duplicate others' offerings? How can you make your work distinct?

SOMEONE WHO DID THIS: Mai didn't have to undertake a big career shift to achieve a big jump in her level of satisfaction and fulfillment.

A super-successful public accountant, Mai rose through the ranks at one of the region's largest public accounting firms. Two years to Audit Senior, a year to Audit Supervisor, two to Audit Manager, and five more to Partner. Along the way, Mai picked up an MBA with a concentration in Finance.

Other than excessive hours during tax season, there was nothing Mai didn't like about her work. She loved solving complex problems for her clients and providing them with tools to make the best decisions. She was comfortable with her role as Partner and helping bring in business was no problem at all.

Mai's firm encouraged Partners to support the community by joining nonprofit boards. Mai was drawn to organizations supporting women and children, and over the years, she served on the boards of a women's shelter and another group providing free childcare to low-income families.

Over time, even though Mai continued to enjoy her role at the accounting firm, she felt drawn more and more to the work of her nonprofit clients at the firm and the nonprofit organizations where she served as a board member.

Mai asked herself an all-important question: Could she do more of this type of work?

Mai confided in a handful of people whose opinion mattered to her. She began to think that the best way to continue in accounting and finance while engaging with mission-driven organizations was to become a consultant to nonprofits.

A year later, Mai launched her practice. She already had contacts in the nonprofit sector, and she immediately reached out to them to say she was open for business. She attended nonprofit events and advertised in vendor listings of the state nonprofit association. She developed a free monthly breakfast series called "Smart Accounting Practices for Smart Organizations" that was always well-attended and highly rated.

From accounting firm to accounting consultant—it's not a huge leap, but the change was significant for Mai. Last time I heard from her she was deep in projects with several nonprofit clients. Her expertise led to her involvement in broader consulting and strategic planning, and Mai could really see her work making a difference. Was the jump to consulting the right decision? "One hundred and ten percent!!" she says.

Make the Jump 7: Teach

Share what you know.

WHAT THIS MEANS: You're hired to teach or train others. At the same time, you continue your own education in the field to become a thought leader. You could write and publish. You could speak.

Work in teaching could be full-time or part-time (adjunct), regular or occasional. The options include graduate level studies, university courses, online college courses, weekend seminars, evening programs, or any combination of the above. If you have a terminal degree, you could work with individual doctoral students or guest lecture to a large undergraduate audience.

Don't limit yourself to post-high school, either. Any interest in returning to school to obtain certifications to teach high school—or middle or elementary school?

Many states have opportunities for trained, experienced industry professionals to quickly gain certifications required to teach in public systems.

If that sounds onerous but you like the idea of teaching younger students, consider engaging with nonprofit organizations supporting student learning. In my area, for example, several nonprofits send trained volunteers into schools to share mini seminars on topics ranging from self-esteem to teamwork/collaboration and conflict management.

If you prefer a less formal role, you could jump into volunteer opportunities with a teaching/training component. The Red Cross, for example, offers scores of training courses from babysitting skills for teens to first aid training. These sessions are staffed by well-trained volunteers.

WHAT YOU'LL NEED: If you choose to teach in a school or university, you'll need the qualifications dictated by the institution and its governing bodies. Your experience counts for a lot but inquire with experts at the types of institutions where you wish to work. They'll help you understand what additional training or other formalities are needed.

If you're strongly considering this option, you probably have a sense of your comfort level in front of a classroom. If you're uncomfortable speaking in front of people, consider teaching online. Do you like to present information but want to bolster your ease up front? Check out Toastmasters or other training in public speaking.

If you're not seeking a formal teaching position in an academic setting, you might need less than you think to start on this path. Most nonprofit organizations with volunteer or paid opportunities to provide training will give you the tools and information you need.

Think about what you like, where you have expertise, and in what type of setting you would wish to share. You're on your way!

SOMEONE WHO DID THIS: Ronald spent his career in various operations leadership positions, rising to be VP of Operations and Logistics for a company manufacturing safety equipment for the construction trades.

With seven children at home, Ronald had little time for traditional volunteer experiences with nonprofit boards and community groups. He never even joined the professional association associated with his industry.

During the many years I've known Ronald, however, I've seen him consistently volunteer for school clubs, youth sports, music groups, and YMCA camps. Indeed, any group or team associated with any of his brood could count on Ronald to say yes to a volunteer position. With seven active youngsters, there was plenty on Ronald's plate.

I've watched him over two decades, amazed, as he seamlessly pulled together career and family. I was surprised 10 years ago when Ronald said he wanted to go back to college. I reminded him that he already had an MBA to complement his 20-plus years of career experience. Ronald agreed, but added that becoming an empty nester was closing in. That fact, and an increasingly strong desire to advance his education, nudged him toward PhD programs.

A year or so went by before I checked in again with Ronald. He was indeed enrolled in a PhD program through an accredited online university, pursuing a doctorate in management. How fantastic! Ronald had further determined that after graduation he would pursue the final chapter of his career—in teaching. Not just any teaching role would do. He wanted to teach at the graduate level at a large public university.

You know what? He did it! After four years in the program, Ronald graduated. He wrote a competent dissertation examining factors surrounding executive leadership of quality control programs in manufacturing firms working with US military contracts. As Ronald's official retirement from his company approached, he inked a deal to become a professor at a large state college. Here was an opportunity to combine his years of practical experience in the business world, his love of sharing and teaching, and his dogged determination to make his dream a reality.

Make the Jump 8: Portfolio Career

Find the perfect mix of what you love to do.

WHAT THIS MEANS: This decision—means you don't have to make a decision!

Would you like to keep your hand in a for-profit organization? Go ahead! Would you like to add a nonprofit gig on a part-time basis? Sure! Would you like to volunteer? Be on a board? Keep some amount of your time open for consulting or interim gigs? It's all on the table.

Your career is your own.
A portfolio career is creating an assortment of activities and roles that uniquely fit you.

WHAT YOU'LL NEED: Indubitably, a sense of adventure. Along with an embrace of ambiguity. With every option on the table, you have literally millions of ways to craft a portfolio career.

Whatever works—works! That said, there's nothing lazy or haphazard about a sustainable portfolio career.

So dig deep.

- What components could you combined to make the richest life?

- What appeals to you most—jobs, volunteerism, hobbies, family, friends? In each category, what are you looking for?

- What do you like to do best?

- Do you prefer to do familiar things or something completely fresh—or a combination?

Think about logistics.

- Do you need to earn an income? How much? How does that figure expand or limit your choices in a portfolio arrangement?

- Do you need employer-provided health insurance or any of the other perks typically provided as employee benefits? Will you need to—and can you afford to—acquire these on your own?

- Portfolio careers might include more than one formal activity. Can you go from place to place if necessary? Is transportation a factor—whether that's a plane, train, or automobile?

SOMEONE WHO DID THIS: My professional colleague Deven is a great example of carving out a portfolio life.

The majority of Deven's professional career consisted of leadership in customer service and later, customer experience, in pharmacy benefit management. On the side, Deven has an active interest in outdoor activities, particularly canoeing and kayaking. He was also a swimming and lifesaving skills instructor.

As Deven approached traditional retirement age, he began thinking creatively. He liked the idea of keeping a regular paid job, although he leaned toward a part-time role. Deven knew he really valued—needed—peers and fellow employees around him. The interactions were indispensable to his sense of belonging and well-being. Yet he wished to continue swimming instruction and even add courses, if possible. Then there was the friend who recently invited Deven to join him in handcrafting a cedar strip canoe.

Deven was fortunate. His organization gave him flexibility with his retirement date. He poked around the nonprofit sector for a few months before obtaining a consistent part-time position at a local park and rec center. He didn't take the suggested six-month break after leaving his corporate job—although later he admitted he wished he had. Rather, he happily started as Recreation Coordinator just two weeks after his retirement party.

A few months later, Deven signed on as a lead instructor in water safety and swimming at the YMCA. And he and his friend built not one but two beautiful cedar strip canoes. Even with everything on his plate, Deven brags he is canoeing twice as often as he did in years past.

I, too, plan for a portfolio life in the not-so-distant future. I value work and plan to maintain a part-time role in my business. But other activities also matter to me, and I want to formalize how I commit time to those as well. That includes carving out time for playing piano and continuing piano lessons as well as spending more time gardening. I'll continue to serve on nonprofit boards. Maybe I'll teach again at the university level.

The final planning for my portfolio career? To be continued…and that's the beauty of it!

Make the Jump 9: Career Shift

Take a pay cut, leave the business world behind.

WHAT THIS MEANS: Much of this book has been about career shift as a way to make the jump to nonprofit.

Many leaders consider a career shift from a full-time corporate executive job to a full-time nonprofit executive job as a highly desirable option. Or perhaps their only option.

By using the techniques and approaches we've discussed in this book, it's possible to shift to a new role that fits both you and the nonprofit organization.

WHAT YOU'LL NEED: Take to heart the suggestions from this book to understand and approach the nonprofit job marketplace.

- You'll need to know enough about the nonprofit sector to determine which jobs in what organizations would best fit you.

- You'll need to have your resume and other written materials ready to present yourself with competence and humility in equal measure.

- You'll need to be able to confidently express your narrative, including the "why" of your interest in a different and perhaps lower-level job than what you've held.

SOMEONE WHO DID THIS: We've already discussed many business-people who successfully transitioned to the nonprofit sector.

My friend Kyle is another.

Kyle's professional career in financial services culminated in a role as a partner/leader at an organization doing mezzanine financing. No, I don't know what exactly what that is, except that it usually has nothing to do with theaters or stadiums. After a few years of 60-plus hour weeks and incessant travel, Kyle began questioning his commitment to the sector where he had worked for so long and so hard.

A handful of thoroughly difficult client situations caused Kyle to think about making a significant change. The only problem? He didn't have much of an idea about what that change might be.

Kyle just knew it would be something very different. And he was intrigued by the nonprofit world.

He asked if I would work with him as he stepped into this largely unknown territory. I said yes—enthusiastically. Although it can be difficult to consult with friends, Kyle has sensitivity matched with tenacity, which I knew would be a winning combination for him in this situation.

We started by pausing. Kyle needed time and space to reflect. We spent time talking. Mostly, I listened. About his interests.

- What parts of his job did he find most gratifying?

- Most challenging?

- What interests were not being met in his current job that could be met in another?

We used interest inventories to guide our conversations and put vocabulary to our findings. We learned that Kyle was beyond ready to leave behind his frenetic pace and charged client situations. We also learned he wanted to continue to work for a mid-sized organization. He enjoyed being hands-on but also preferred complexity and scope. His initial thought was to go for a top-level leadership role, but he was open.

Like many corporate executives, scheduling had precluded Kyle from having time for as many volunteer assignments as he may have liked. To be ready to assess his options, Kyle needed to know more. He didn't have a rich sense of the nonprofit sector in his region, and he wasn't entirely sure where to plug in.

So we devised a plan for nonprofit immersion.

We assigned Kyle a two-month preparation phase. During this phase, he would set about gaining the knowledge and connections he would need to begin approaching nonprofit organizations about potential roles. At first, he did a ton of reading—books, articles, websites, blogs, anything related to nonprofit work that caught his attention. We created formal activities for him during this phase, but we also allowed him to spend time following his heart and interests to various sources.

Once armed with a better sense of the nonprofit landscape, Kyle was ready to begin getting input from personal and professional contacts with experience and perspectives about the nonprofit sector. Specifically, he hoped to learn where his network could envision him applying his background and skills in fresh ways.

Kyle proved to be an able networker. With every successive meeting, he felt more energized and confident. He started to picture how he could keep what he loved about work and at the same time make an impact.

As Kyle launched into networking, we began working on his written materials. We spruced up his resume, created a one-page marketing document, and a formal bio just in case.

We decided not to apply for jobs online. Nor did we contact any recruiters.

It was a slightly radical decision, but we knew that approaching the non-profit job market through those avenues put us in tough competition with large applicant pools likely full of highly qualified candidates. Kyle liked meeting people and his network was full of contacts with deep connections in the nonprofit space.

We liked Kyle's odds better via networking.

There were several nifty opportunities Kyle interviewed for. Generally, Kyle was well received by hiring executives and committees, but he didn't come out on top in all situations. A couple early interviews were bumpy. Particularly, Kyle felt he was struggling with those questions around "Why?"

- "Why are you interested in changing sectors at this point in your career?"

- "Why would you want to take a step down in overall responsibility?"

- "Do you *know* what this job entails?"

- "Why are you interested in our work?"

It wasn't that Kyle was dishonest in his answers. He wasn't. But even as he answered these questions, albeit truthfully, he felt his words and demeanor came across as nervous or uncertain. We role played these questions to work out bugs.

Fast forward a few more months, and Kyle had not one but two worthy employment offers from nonprofit organizations. The offers were similar—title, compensation range, size of organization. However, they came from two entirely different parts of the sector, both of which had great interest for Kyle.

After reflection and advice from mentors, Kyle accepted an offer to become the Finance Manager at a county historical society in the area where he resides. While not the "top job," it was interesting and fit the bill for Kyle. Six months later, Kyle confirmed he had made the right decision. The effort to intentionally make a career change was worth it! He was liking his job and loving life.

Make the Jump 10: Start a Nonprofit

Use your passion to create your own organization.

WHAT THIS MEANS: You become the founder of a new nonprofit organization.

You have a passion for a particular mission. You've done a deep dive into the existing services or programs related to your mission and you can't find that the community need is adequately or specifically met at this time. You've networked, studied the market, and done all due diligence. You conclude that doing this work connected to another organization or in another way does not make sense.

You discern that you have ideas, passion, strategy, and means to create a nonprofit to serve this need.

Perhaps you'll do this with others. Or maybe you'll create the organization alone.

WHAT YOU'LL NEED: Realistic assessment of need.

- What exactly will your nonprofit organization do or provide?

- Is this offering provided elsewhere?

- Is a similar or related offering provided elsewhere—so that you're inviting confusion and competition?

- Could another organization do this better? More cost effectively? More quickly?

These are just a start of questions for you to ponder.

What compels you to start a nonprofit? If it's only because you haven't landed a nonprofit job, stop now.

That's no reason to create a nonprofit.

Hear me out. The world has a staggering number of nonprofit organizations. Most are very small—under $3M in revenue. Each requires staff to perform the programmatic service work, but each also requires personnel to perform administration, accounting, fundraising, and other work duplicated again and again across every organization. For all the numerous tiny nonprofits doing similar things, there are no economies of scale.

Most newly formed nonprofit organizations don't last more than five years. Of those that survive, many face chronic financial shortfalls and other predictable struggles.

With few exceptions, the world doesn't need another nonprofit organization.

Tough words, I know. But I say them to encourage you to stop and assess whether the absolute best way to accomplish your mission is by creating another organization. And I'll share the story of a friend who found it necessary.

Still interested in founding a nonprofit? Okay, let's proceed.

There are many things you'll need to successfully launch. This list details just a few critical components.

- **Needs analysis and strategic planning.** At the very beginning, you'll need to drill down to exactly *why* your organization needs to exist. Use as much information as you can find—demographic data, population data, information about existing related services in your area. **Ask:** What community need will the organization address? What population will it serve? Why is this needed? Is any other organization meeting this need?

Start your organization with clear strategic thinking and planning. Tightly define the mission and vision of the organization. Invite others, including your board of directors and outside experts, to help you think this through from start to finish and all the hard parts in-between.

As with a for-profit organization, the mission and strategy should lead to a sound business plan. Create documents with specific details of how the organization will achieve it mission. Set goals. Set timelines. Set measurements.

- **Time.** You'll need a lot of time to start a nonprofit. Think full-time job time. Or more. Can you commit to that?

- **Support.** You'll face roadblocks and barriers. Not everyone will share your focus and enthusiasm. How will you fortify yourself when the going gets tough? What's your support system to encourage you to keep going? Who will pitch in to financially support the enterprise if requested?

- **Legal and financial acumen and assistance.** You'll need legal advice and assistance to create a new organization. It's possible you could use online legal resources to create a small, simple organization. But most of the time, it makes sense to engage legal counsel. There are Articles of Incorporation to prepare. You need an EIN (Employer Identification Number) from the Internal Revenue Service via Form SS4. You need to secure 501 (c) (3) exemption, a state tax exemption, and a charity solicitation registration. You'll need a charter and bylaws.

You'll also need financial assistance. Depending on the organization's complexity and your own expertise, you'll likely need outside expertise to set up bookkeeping and accounting.

And there's the ongoing work. Who will do the detailed financial work? Will this be outsourced? Will you hire someone?

- **Funding.** Your biggest challenge will likely be how to fund this new organization. Grants are available—you'll need skills in grant writing or someone to assist you—but money often isn't given to start-ups. Will you provide services government entities will pay for? How will you obtain contracts for your services? How will you measure progress and maintain funding?

Fundraising is a part of the revenue streams for most nonprofits. How will you raise money? Friends and family? Broader community? Fundraising takes time. Even a superior fundraising strategy doesn't count on significant payout for two or three years. How will you put forward a sustained fundraising initiative while securing revenue elsewhere?

- **Board of directors.** You will likely be required to have a Board of Directors (check with the Attorney General's office in your state). These board members could be your family and close friends, or expand to include experts in various disciplines. However, successful nonprofit leaders almost universally say they rely heavily on the advice and assistance of a board of directors.

If you're not ready for a formal board, could you assemble a less formal advisory council?

- Who do you know that shares your passion for this mission?

- Who might offer valuable advice and counsel?

- Who would commit time to this endeavor?

- Who would actively participate with a combination of positivity and willingness to call out something that needs to change?

Study the board makeup of several nonprofit organizations and talk to several board members. Figure out how this resource would work for you.

- **Marketing and Communications.** Eventually you'll choose a name for the organization and a brand image. How will you communicate about your new organization? Who needs to hear? How will you reach them? Will you engage a consultant to work on marketing and communications? Will you hire someone or do this yourself?

- **Staffing and Human Resources.** Unless you're considering being a one-person shop, you'll need to hire staff. Will your organization be large enough that eventually you'll need a management team? How strong is your background in talent acquisition? How will you determine compensation and benefits? You'll need to develop organizational policies and perhaps an Employee Handbook. Who will assist?

The above information is just a short overview of what's needed to start and sustain a nonprofit organization. Please seek out expert

resources—particularly legal, financial, and philanthropic—as you begin this endeavor.

SOMEONE WHO DID THIS: I got to know Harry through the board of a local organization serving individuals with disabilities. His business career had been in transportation management, from railroad to trucking logistics management. He eventually rose to Chief Operations Officer at the company where he spent 37 years.

Harry had always been an active community volunteer, and after retiring from business, he began serving on several boards and committees of statewide organizations advocating for individuals with disabilities. We crossed paths when I gave a presentation on succession planning to a board where Harry served. His fellow board members commented on his tireless devotion to the work.

I was impressed enough with Harry's dedication to that nonprofit organization. Then I learned Harry was also the founder of a nonprofit himself.

As many others do, Harry founded a nonprofit to serve the unmet need of a family member. In this case, it was Harry's children.

Along with his wife Regina, Harry had two adult daughters with developmental disabilities. As the girls grew up, Harry and Regina began to worry about where they might live after high school. Each daughter had a job in their community and enjoyed a level of independence. Still, each daughter required support.

Harry, of course, went hunting for resources to meet his daughters' needs. He used his network to investigate residential programs available to his daughters. They had the challenge of living in a smaller community, where there were no residential facilities within 40 miles of their home capable of meeting their daughters' needs. Harry and his wife supported their daughters' wish for independence, but they also wanted to live within a reasonable driving distance.

So Harry started a nonprofit residence to serve adults with developmental disabilities right in his community. I'm not familiar with all that Harry did to launch this nonprofit but I imagine it was a mountain of work. Harry and his wife acted as the original board of directors and purchased a fourplex with a large backyard and big maple tree in the front. They hired an executive director with a clinical background to run the physical complex, hire and manage a small staff, and oversee programs.

Today, with a second location added, Maple House provides supportive housing for up to 12 residents who identify as female. A small staff gives assistance with chores and daily living and helps residents with transportation to their jobs.

Other community leaders have since joined Harry and Regina on the board of Maple House. Many are fellow parents of residents. This small nonprofit was founded by parents with a passion for securing the best resources for their children, and it continues to meet a special need.

Last Word

So where are you at in the process of making your jump to a nonprofit job?

- If you're just starting to think about making the jump—great! Continue to use this book to help you assess what's possible. Think about all your options. Use the recommendations in the book to follow your dreams.

- If you're actively in the process of seeking a nonprofit role—terrific! Have you learned anything new about how you might approach that task? What could you do differently? If your original plan isn't coming together, perhaps you now see equally fulfilling alternatives.

- If you've made the jump—congratulations! You're on your way. I wish you continued joy, energy, and perseverance in your new role. Stay active. Stay current. Stay connected.

Whatever your situation, I applaud your interest in pursuing a new career direction in the nonprofit sector.

My final word: Remember why you picked up this book—to do the hard and rewarding work of impacting lives. The world can't get enough good people responding to their best impulses, and I hope you will bring others along on your journey wherever it leads.

To all readers of this book, please accept my best wishes for your continued success.

Marcia Ballinger
Fall 2021

Acknowledgements

Writing a book is certainly a very individual and often isolating venture. And at the same time, it is a collective effort that relies on the voices and talents of many in order to succeed. I am so incredibly grateful for the guidance and input of many extraordinary people in my life.

My colleagues at Ballinger|Leafblad are the absolute best. Thank you to Lars Leafblad, Jen Hanlon Ash, Jill Harmon, Holly Kelsey Henry, Bob Schoenbaum, Diane Schwecke, and Damon Shoholm.

Loud shout outs to Kevin Johnson, uber-talented book coach and Richard Dodson, master coordinator of edits, book design, and marketing.

Much appreciation to my friend Karen Kodzik at Cultivating Careers for her listening ear and feedback.

Thanks upon thanks to George Dow, my personal career coach. His wisdom and guidance continue to be life changing.

Sincere gratitude to industry leaders Nancy Burke and Kate Barr for sharing their expertise and perspectives.

Finally, and most importantly, my profound gratitude to those individuals who have contacted me over the years to confide their interest in the nonprofit sector, to share their stories, to seek my insights, and to include me in their career journeys.

About the Author

Marcia Ballinger is Co-Founder and Principal at Ballinger|Leafblad, a national executive search firm based in the Twin Cities. She has over 25 years of experience in the executive recruiting field serving both nonprofit and corporate sectors.

Marcia has a BS in Business Administration and an MA in Speech-Communication along with a PhD in Organization and Management from Capella University where she later served as chair of the board of directors. An active community leader, Marcia lives with her husband Brad in St Paul. They have one adult daughter and two dogs.

Marcia is the author of *The 20-Minute Networking Meeting*, and *Winning the Executive Interview*.

Made in United States
Orlando, FL
28 February 2022

15246098R00109